THE LETTER - WRITER'S
Companion and Address Book

ANGUS & ROBERTSON PUBLISHERS

Forms of Address

Many persons of rank or professional prominence require special forms of address. Listed here are those thought most useful to Australian letter writers.

Royalty

The Queen, Prince Philip and members of the Royal Family

Other than for formal or state documents correspondence to the Queen should be addressed to "The Private Secretary to Her Majesty The Queen". In such correspondence the first reference to the Queen should be as "Her Majesty", subsequent ones as "The Queen".

Prince Philip and all royal children are styled as "His (or Her) Royal Highness" in the first reference and "The Duke of . . .", "Prince . . ." and so on, in subsequent ones.

Orders of Chivalry

Knight

Address: "Sir (William) . . ." plus the recognised letters of the Order, for example K.T. or G.B.E. or K.B.E.
Salutation: "Dear Sir (William)".

Knight Bachelor

As above but without letters following the name.

Local Government

Lord Mayor

(Use the same form of address for both men and women)

Address: "The Right Hon. the Lord Mayor of . . ., Alderman . . . . . ." (Sydney, Hobart, Brisbane); "The Right Hon. the Lord Mayor of Melbourne, Councillor . . . . . ." (Melbourne); "The Right Hon. the Lord Mayor of . . ., Mr . . . . . ." (Adelaide and Perth); "The Right Worshipful Lord Mayor of Darwin, Mr . . . . . ." (Darwin); "The Right Worshipful the Lord Mayor of . . ., Alderman . . . . . ." (Geelong, Newcastle, Wollongong).
Salutation: "Dear Lord Mayor".

Mayor

Address: "His worship the Mayor of . . .", Alderman (Councillor) . . . . . .".
Salutation: "Dear Mayor".

Shire President

Address: "The Shire President, Councillor . . .".
Salutation: "Dear Mr President".

Alderman

Address: "Alderman . . . . . .".
Salutation: "Alderman".

"Writing Home", a postcard of Australian bush life attributed to J. Hutchings whose work was popular early this century and is widely collected today.

Government

Governor-General *Address:* "His Excellency Sir (or Mr) . . . . . .".
Salutation: "Your Excellency" or "My dear Governor-General".

Governor *Address:* "His Excellency Sir (or Mr) . . . . . .".
Salutation: "Your Excellency" or "My dear Governor".

Dame *Address:* "Dame (Obelia) . . ." plus the initials of the Order, for example G.C.B. or D.C.B. or D.C.V.O.
Salutation: "Dear Dame (Obelia)".

NOTE: In addressing Knights and Dames of the Order of Australia use A.K. and A.D. respectively after their names but the Order eschews the preceding titles "Sir" and "Dame".

Prime Minister *Address:* "The (Right) Hon. . . . ., M.P., Prime Minister".
Salutation: "Dear Prime Minister" or "My dear Prime Minister".

Minister, Senate or House of Representatives *Address:* "Senator the (Right) Hon. . . . . Minister for . . ." or "The (Right) Hon. . . . ., M.P., Minister for . . .".
Salutations: "Dear Minister".

Senator *Address:* "Senator the (Right) Hon. . . . .".
Salutation: "Dear Senator".

Member, House of Representatives *Address:* "Mr (or, if a member of the Privy Council or a former Minister, the Right Hon.) . . . ., M.P.".
Salutation: "Dear Mr . . .".

Premier *Address:* "The Hon. . . . ., M.P. (or in South Australia M.H.A.), Premier of . . .".
Salutation: "Dear Mr Premier".

State Minister *Address:* "The Hon. . . . ., M.P. (M.L.A. or M.H.A. as appropriate), Minister for . . .".
Salutation: "Dear Mr . . .".

Member, Legislative Council *Address:* "The Hon. . . . ., M.L.C.".
Salutation: "Dear Mr . . .".

Member, Legislative Assembly or House of Assembly (S.A.) *Address:* "Mr . . . . . . (M.P., M.L.A. or M.H.A. as appropriate)".
Salutation: "Dear Mr . . .".

Clergy

Archbishop,
Anglican or Roman Catholic

Address: "The Most Rev. The Archbishop of . . ." or "His Grace, The Most Reverend . . . . . ., Archbishop of . . .".
Salutation: "Your Grace" or "Dear Archbishop".

Cardinal

Address: "His Eminence, Cardinal . . . . . . (or, if knighted, "His Eminence, Cardinal Sir . . . . . ."), Archbishop of . . .". (No letters are added after the name as the title Cardinal embraces all others.)
Salutation: "Your Eminence" or "Dear Cardinal . . .".

Bishop

Address: "The Right Rev. . . . ., the Bishop of . . .".
Salutation: "Dear Bishop".

Bishop
(Roman Catholic)

Address: "His Lordship, The Most Rev. . . . . . . (initials), Bishop of . . .".
Salutation: "My Lord".

Moderator-General and Moderators of State Assemblies of the Presbyterian Church

Address: "The Right Reverend . . . . . .".
Salutation: "Dear Sir", "Reverend Sir" or "Dear Mr . . .".

President and State Moderators of the Uniting Church

Address: "The Reverend . . . . . .".
Salutation: "Dear Mr . . .".

Minister, Deacon, Curate, Priest

Address: "The Reverend . . . . . .".
Salutation: "Dear Mr . . .".

Priest
(Roman Catholic)

Address: "The Reverend Father . . . . . .".
Salutation: "Dear Father . . .".

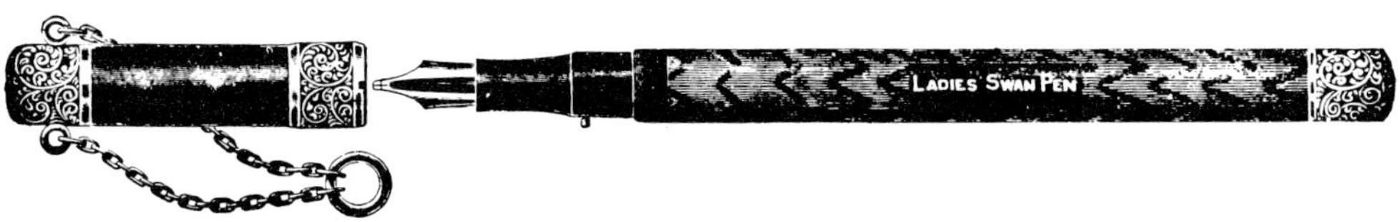

CHRISTMAS CARD LIST

Christmas stamps issued in 1982 and featuring early Australian Christmas cards. These were among the first Christmas cards designed and printed in Australia in 1881.

A

Telephone:

Telephone:

Telephone:

Telephone:

Telephone:

'Reaping', one of a series of postcards depicting Australian life, c. 1905 by J. Hutchings.

Telephone:

A

An Early Correspondent

Among the treasured records of the First Fleet are the writings of Ralph Clarke, a young officer who in much of what he wrote addresses his "Beloved Betsy":

> "9 oClock Saw the Supply Brigg in Botany Bay at Anchor . . . thanks to my good and Gracious God for his kindness to your Ralph in preserving me in health and welfare and from the dangers of the Sea . . . oh my Beloved Betsey return thanks and Prayers to him for his kindness to me and I hope that he will befriend me still—I cannot Say from the appearance of the Shore that I will like it the only thing I ask is that it may be a healthy place."

Telephone:

Telephone:

Telephone:

Telephone:

Telephone:

Telephone:

A

A

Telephone:

Telephone:

Telephone:

Telephone:

Telephone:

Telephone:

B

FROM *OLD JOHN BAX*

"Tan-tan-ta-ra, boys! Here comes the mail,
Rolling down the cleared line, sun, rain, or hail!
Rocking up the main street, as hard as she can go!"
When Old John Bax drove the coach for Cobb and Co.

D. H. SOUTER

Telephone:

Telephone:

Telephone:

Telephone:

Telephone:

Telephone:

B

Telephone:

Telephone:

Telephone:

Telephone:

Telephone:

Telephone:

"Collecting the Mail", a postcard by A. H. Fullwood published about 1905. Fullwood was one of the main illustrators of the *Picturesque Atlas of Australia* published in 1888 and his many postcards, published by Raphael Tuck & Sons in the "Wide-Wide-World" series of Oilettes, are similar to the *Atlas* illustrations.

B

Embossed Correspondence

In 1838 the first overland mail service in Australia was effected between Sydney and Melbourne. Embossed postage covers were introduced in Sydney for 1s 3d per dozen. This was the first time in the world that a system of prepayment of postage by means of a stamped letter became available.

Telephone:

Telephone:

Telephone:

Telephone:

Telephone:

Telephone:

Telephone:

Telephone:

C

"We Deliver"

The Post Office had its beginning in Australia in 1809 when Isaac Nichols, Assistant to the Naval Officer in Sydney, was appointed to board vessels and receive inward mails. Additionally, an office was established at his house in George Street (second from left in the illustration) to receive all letters and parcels addressed to inhabitants of the Colony of New South Wales.

Upon delivery, recipients were required to pay charges ranging from 1s (10c) for each letter to 5s (50c) for a parcel weighing more than 20 lbs (9 kg).

The date of the relevant government order, 25 April 1809, is regarded as the foundation day of today's Australia Post.

In 1810, a year later, Nichols was appointed an official Postmaster and the delivery charges on letters and parcels were greatly reduced.

C

AN OFFICIAL LETTER

Part of a dispatch sent by Sir Charles FitzRoy, Governor of New South Wales to the British Secretary of State:

May 22, 1851

MY LORD,

I avail myself of a private opportunity which has unexpectedly offered, and by which a letter is likely to reach your Lordship quickly, to inform you of a discovery of gold in that part of this Colony which lies to the westward of the town of Bathurst, and the nearest point of which is about 150 miles from Sydney.

. . . I have not deemed it advisable to increase the very great excitement which is engrossing and unhinging the minds of all classes of the community, by taking such steps as will be necessary for asserting the rights of the Crown over the proceeds of the gold field without obtaining further confirmation of its extent and value . . .

I have, etc . . .

C.A. FitzRoy

Telephone:

Telephone:

Telephone:

Telephone:

Telephone:

Telephone:

Gold Diggers Receiving a Letter from Home:
William Strutt

C

Envelopes and Alternatives

Letters

To attract the minimum postage rates letters should be sent in envelopes that are Post Office Preferred. They should be:

no smaller than 88 mm × 138 mm and
no larger than 122 mm × 237 mm

Postcards

The postage fee for postcards, whether sent airmail overseas or within Australia, depends on the size. Aerograms are charged at a standard rate which is generally less than for overseas-bound postcards and standard letters.

Christmas cards

Special low rates are announced each year for Christmas cards sent in a Post Office Preferred envelope. "Card Only" should be written on the left hand front of the envelope.

Telephone:

Telephone:

Telephone:

Telephone:

Telephone:

Telephone:

Telephone:

Telephone:

Telephone:

C

MAIL BY RAIL

In 1855 the first transportation of mail by rail in Australia was between Sydney and Parramatta.

The Arrival of the First Train from Parramatta from the *Illustrated Sydney News*

Kitty McCrae

The western sun, ere he sought his lair,
Skimmed the treetops, and, glancing thence,
Rested awhile on the curling hair
Of Kitty McCrae, by the boundary fence:
Her eyes looked anxious; her cheeks were pale;
For father was two hours late with the mail.

Never before had he been so late;
And Kitty wondered and wished him back,
Leaning athwart the big swing gate
That opens out on the bridle-track—
A tortuous path that sidles down
From the single street of a mining town.

But now, in the shadows' deepening
When the last sun-spark has ceased to burn,
Afar she catches the sullen ring
Of horse-hoofs swinging around the turn;
Then painfully down the narrow trail
Comes Alec McCrae with the Greytown mail.

"The fever-and-ague, my girl," he said—
" 'Twas all I got on that northern trip:
When it left me then I was well-nigh dead—
Has got me fast in its iron grip;
And I'd rather rot in the nearest gaol
Than ride to-night with the Greytown mail.

"At Golden Gully they heard to-day—
'Twas a common topic about the town—
That the Mulligan Gang were around this way.
They wouldn't despatch the gold-dust down;
And Brown, the manager, said he thought
'Twere wise to wait for a strong escort.

"I rode the leaders; the other nags
I left with the coach at the 'Travellers' Rest.'
Kitty, my lass, you must take the bags—
Postboy, I reckon's about the best;
'Tis dark, I know, but he'll never fail
To take you down with the Greytown mail."

It needed no further voice to urge
This dutiful daughter to eager haste;
She donned the habit of rough blue serge
That draped itself from her slender waist;
And Postboy stood by the stockyard rail
While she mounted behind the Greytown mail.

Dark points, the rest of him iron-grey,
Boasting no strain of expensive blood,
Down steepest hill he could pick his way,
And never was baulked by a winter flood—
Strong as a lion, hard as a nail,
Was the horse that carried the Greytown mail.

And Postboy's bosom was filled with pride
As he felt the form of his mistress sway,
In its easy grace, to his swinging stride
As he dashed along down the narrow way.
No prettier Mercury, I'll go bail,
Than Kitty e'er carried a Government mail.

Sidling the Range by a narrow path
Where towering mountain-ash trees grow,
And a slip meant more than an icy bath
In the tumbling waters that foamed below;
Through the white fog filling each silent vale
Rode Kitty McCrae with the Greytown mail.

The forest shadows became less dense:
They fairly flew down the river fall:
When out from the shade of an old brush-fence
Stepped three armed men with a sudden call.
Sharp and stern came the well-known hail:
"Stand! for we want the Greytown mail!"

Postboy swerved with a mighty bound
As an outlaw clung to his bridle rein:
A hoof-stroke flattened him to the ground
With a curse that was half a cry of pain;
While Kitty, trembling and rather pale
Rode for life and the Greytown mail.

To save the bags was her only thought
As she bent to the whistle of angry lead
That followed the flash and the sharp report;
But, "Oh, you cowards!" was all she said.
Fast through the storm of leaden hail
Kitty rode on with the Greytown mail.

Safe? Ah no! for a tiny stream
On Postboy's coat left its crimson mark.
She still rode on; but 'twas in a dream,
Through lands where shadows fell drear and dark:
Like a wounded sea-bird before the gale
Fled Kitty McCrae with the Greytown mail.

And ever the crimson life-stream drips—
For every hoof-stroke a drop of blood—
From feeble fingers the bridle slips
As down the Warrigal Flat they scud;
And just where the Redbank workings lie
She reels and falls with a feeble cry.

The old horse slackened his racing pace
When he found the saddle his only load,
And laid his nose to the pretty face
White upturned in the dusty road;
Like a gathered rose in the heat of day,
So drooped and faded Kitty McCrae.

Did Postboy stay by the dead girl's side?
Not he! relieved of her feather-weight,
He woke the echoes with measured stride,
Galloping up to the postal gate—
Blood, dust, and sweat from head to tail,
A riderless horse with the Greytown mail!

And now a river-oak, drooping, weeps
In ceaseless sorrow above the grave
Down on the flat where Kitty sleeps,
Hushed by the river's lapping wave—
That ever tells to the trees the tale
Of how she rode with the Greytown mail.

BARCROFT BOAKE

Attacking the Mail: *S. T. Gill 1854*

D

Telephone:

Telephone:

Telephone:

Telephone:

Telephone:

Telephone:

Come-By-Chance

As I pondered very weary o'er a volume long and
dreary—
For the plot was void of interest—'twas that Postal
Guide, in fact,
There I learnt the true location, distance, size, and
population
Of each township, town, and village in the radius
of the Act.

And I learnt that Puckawidgee stands beside the
Murrumbidgee,
And that Booleroi and Bumble get their letters twice
a year,
Also that the post inspector, when he visited
Collector,
Closed the office up instanter, and re-opened
Dungalear.

But my languid mood forsook me, when I found a
name that took me,
Quite by chance I came across it—"Come-by-
Chance" was what I read;
No location was assigned it, not a thing to help
one find it,
Just an "N" which stood for northward, and the
rest was all unsaid.

A. B. Paterson

D

D

Telephone:

Telephone:

Telephone:

Telephone:

Telephone:

Telephone:

A Back Blocks Post Office.

A BACK-BLOCKS POST OFFICE.

E

Telephone:

Telephone:

Telephone:

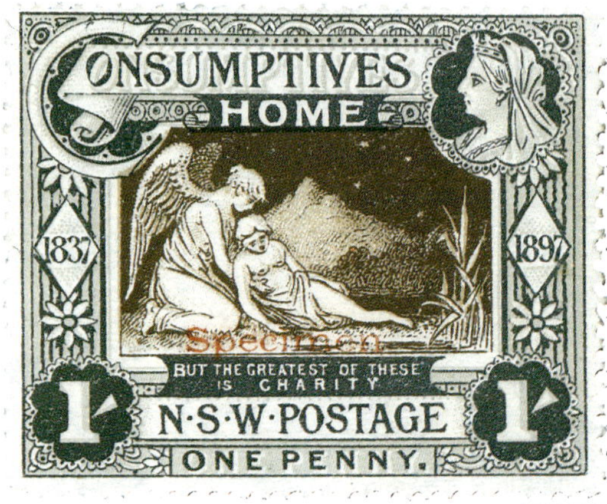

Telephone:

Telephone:

Telephone:

E

Telephone:

Telephone:

Telephone:

Telephone:

Telephone:

Telephone:

E

Beautiful and Unusual

These two "charity" stamps issued in 1897 with postal values of one penny and two pence halfpenny, were sold at post offices for one shilling and two shillings and sixpence respectively. The difference went towards the fund for the TB sufferers' home.

F

THREE MONTHS TO REACH US

EXMOOR,
December 27th 1862

MY DEAREST ETTIE,

I wrote to you last on the ninth of this month. Biddulph took the letters with him to Port Denison, whence he meant to start by the steamer for Brisbane, but after waiting a week in the Port, which he describes as the dullest, hottest and generally most detestable little town he ever saw, it became evident that the steamer had missed this trip, so he came last Monday, to our great surprise, when we thought he was at Rockhampton at least.

The steamer is expected again next week, and he is going off again tomorrow to meet her. I hope he will be more fortunate. It is very inconvenient that the *Murray* is so uncertain, as it is nearly a hundred miles from here to Port Denison. I expect you will get several of my letters together, but if so you must be sure and read those of the earliest date first, and then they will not be so stupid, but will come in the form of a journal.

I am writing now chiefly to acknowledge your seventeenth of September letter, which reached me on the thirteenth of this month. You see, you may reckon on your letters generally taking three months to reach us . . .

YOUR AFFECTIONATE SISTER
Rachel Henning

FROM *THE LETTERS OF RACHEL HENNING*

Telephone:

Telephone:

Telephone:

Telephone:

Telephone:

Telephone:

F

Telephone:

Telephone:

Telephone:

Telephone:

Telephone:

Telephone:

F

Telephone:

Telephone:

Telephone:

Telephone:

Telephone:

Telephone:

F

THE MAILS

The tail-rods leap in their bearings—
  They rise with a rush and ring;
They sink to the sound of laughter,
  And hurried and short they sing—
    We carry the Mails—
    His Majesty's Mails—
  Make way for the Mails of the King!

We've swung her head for the open bay,
  And, spun by the prisoned steam,
The screws are drumming the miles away
  Where the bright star-shadows dream.
She lifts and sways to the ocean's swell;
  The light-house glares on high,
And the fisher-lads in their boats will tell
  How they saw the Mail go by
A-thrill from keel to her quivering spars,
  With the screw-foam boiling white,
And black smoke dimming the watching stars
  As it soared through the soundless night.
"Full speed ahead!" shout the racing rods—
  "Full speed!" and spray on the rail!
We'll heed no order to stop save God's,
  For we are the Ocean Mail.

The big fish shudder to hear the thud
  And stamp of our engine-room,
As we thunder on, with our decks a-flood,
  Through the blind, bewildering gloom.
A faint, hoarse hail, and a waving light—
  The whirr of our steering-gear—
And we are staggering in our flight
  With a fishing-boat just clear.
We carry the wealth of the world, I trow,
  And the power and fame of men,
The angry word, and the lover's vow,
  All held in the turn of a pen.
And stars swing out in the skies a-thrill,
  And the weary stars grow pale;
But night and day we are driving still,
  For we are the Ocean Mail.

Telephone:

Telephone:

Telephone:

G

The sailing craft and the clumsy tramps
Loom up and are lost astern,
And the stars of their bridge and mast-head lamps
Are the only stars that burn.
To the clash and ring of the whirling steel,
And the crash and swing of the seas,
We carry the grief that the mothers feel
As they sob and pray on their knees.
The cares and joys of the throbbing world
Are measured in piston-strokes,
When the bright prow-smother is split and hurled,
And the hot wake steams and smokes.
To the swinging blows of the heavy throws,
And the slide-valves' moaning wail,
We'll swing and soar with our flues a-roar,
For we are the Ocean Mail.

They watch for us at the harbour-mouth,
And wait for us on the quay,
Looking ever to east and south
For our head-light on the sea.
And onward, surging, we're racing fast
Where the shy mermaiden dwells,
And the crested kings of the deep ride past
(Oh! the pomp of the rolling swells).
Lone lighthouse-men, when they see our star
Lift clear of the starry maze,
Will watch us swagger across the bar
And swing to the channelled ways.
Yet never a sign or a sound we give—
No blast of horn or a hail—
For we must race that the world may live,
And we are the Ocean Mail.

The good screws, labouring under,
Laugh loud as they lift and fling
The eddying foam behind them,
And muttering low they sing—
Make way for the Mails—
His Majesty's Mails—
We carry the Mails for the King!

WILL LAWSON

G

The Exclusive Postmistress

Gullgong [sic] was certainly a rough place . . . but not quite so rough as I had expected. There was a hotel there, at which I got a bedroom to myself, though but a small one, and made only of slabs . . . Every habitation and shop had probably required but a few days for its erection . . . Everything needful, however, seemed to be at hand. There were bakers, butchers, grocers, and dealers in soft goods. There were public houses and banks in abundance. There was an auctioneer's establishment . . . There was a photographer, and there was a theatre, at which I saw the "Colleen Bawn" acted with a great deal of spirit . . . After the theatre a munificent banker of the town gave us an oyster supper, at a supper-room . . . I was charmed to hear that a few nights before there had been a most successful public ball. But I was distressed that there had been some heart-burning. Where was the line to be drawn in reference to the ladies? The postmistress would not attend the ball unless barmaids were excluded. The barmaids—I think very properly—were admitted, and the postmistress, who enjoyed the reputation of being the beauty of Gullgong, remained at home.

ANTHONY TROLLOPE
FROM *AUSTRALIA AND NEW ZEALAND*

Telephone:

Telephone:

Telephone:

Telephone:

Telephone:

Telephone:

G

G

Telephone:

Telephone:

Telephone:

Telephone:

Telephone:

Telephone:

"A Bendigo Ball" by C. Abbold, from his *Life on the Diggings*.

THE BUSH MAILMAN

The Fizzer was due at sun-down, and for the Fizzer to be due meant that the Fizzer would arrive; and by six o'clock we had all got cricks in our necks, with trying to go about as usual, and yet keep an expectant eye on the north track.

The Fizzer is unlike every type of man excepting a bush mailman. Hard, sinewy, dauntless, and enduring, he travels day after day and month after month, practically alone—"on me Pat Malone", he calls it—with or without a black boy, according to circumstances, and five trips out of his yearly eight throwing dice with death along his dry stages, and yet at all times as merry as a grig, and as chirrupy as a young grasshopper.

With a light-hearted "So long, chaps," he sets out from the Katherine on his thousand-mile ride, and with a cheery "What ho, chaps! Here we are again!" rides in again within five weeks with that journey behind him.

A thousand miles on horseback "on me Pat Malone", into the Australian interior and out again, travelling twice over three long dry stages and several shorter ones, and keeping strictly within the Government time-limit—if it wasn't a death experience. "Like to see one of 'em doing it 'emselves," says the Fizzer. Yet never a day late, and rarely an hour, he does it eight times a year, with a "So long, chaps", and a "Here we are again".

The Fizzer was due at sun-down, and at sun-down a puff of dust rose on the track, and as a cry of "Mail ho!" went up all round the homestead, the Fizzer rode out of the dust.

"Hullo! What ho, boys!" he shouted in welcome, and the next moment we were in the midst of his clattering team of pack-horses.

For five minutes everything was in confusion; horse bells and hobbles jingling and clanging, harness rattling, as horses shook themselves free, and pack-bags, swags, and saddles came to the ground with loud, creaking flops. Everyone was lending a hand, and the Fizzer, moving in and out among the horses, shouted a medley of news and instructions and welcome.

. . . Then as a pack-bag dropped at the Maluka's feet, he added: "That's the station lot, boss. Full bags, missus! Two on 'em. You'll be doing the disappearing trick in half a mo'."

In "half a mo'" the seals were broken, the mail-matter shaken out on the ground. A cascade of papers, magazines, and books, with a fat, firm little packet of letters among them; forty letters in all—thirty of them falling to my lot—thirty fat, bursting envelopes,

"The Fizzer is unlike every other type of man excepting a bush mail man."

Illustration by Evert Ploeg from *We of the Never-Never* by Mrs Aeneas Gunn.

A Postman Delivering Mail Outback, an 1894 watercolour painting by J. A. Comyns from a private collection.

and in another "half mo'" we had all slipped away in different directions—each with our precious mail matter—doing the "disappearing trick" even to the Fizzer's satisfaction.

The Fizzer smiled amiably after the retreating figures, and then went to be entertained by Cheon. He expected nothing else. He provided feasts all along his route, and was prepared to stand aside while the bush-folk feasted. Perhaps in the silence that fell over the bush homes, after his mail-bags were opened, his own heart slipped away to dear ones, who were waiting somewhere for news of our Fizzer.

Eight mails *only* in a year is not all disadvantage. Townsfolk who have eight hundred tiny doses of mail-matter doled out to them, like men on sick diet, can form little idea of the pleasure of that feast of "full bags and two on 'em", for like thirsty camels we drank it all in—every drop of it—in long deep, satisfying draughts.

It may have been a disadvantage, perhaps, to have been so thirsty; but then only the thirsty soul knows the sweetness of slaking that thirst.

After a full hour's silence the last written sheet was laid down, and I found the Maluka watching and smiling.

"Enjoyed your trip South, little 'un?" he said, and I came back to the bush with a start, to find the supper dead cold. But then supper came every night and the Fizzer once in forty-two.

At daybreak he was at it again, shouting among his horses, as he culled his team of "done-ups", and soon after breakfast was at the head of the south track with all aboard.

"So long, chaps," he called. "See you again half past eleven four weeks"; and by "half past eleven four weeks" he would have carried his precious freight of letters to the yearning, waiting men and women hidden away in the heart of Australia, and be out again, laden with Inside letters for the Outside world.

At all seasons of the year he calls the first two hundred miles of his trip a "kid's game". "Water somewhere nearly every day, and a decent camp most nights." And although he speaks of the next hundred and fifty as being a "bit off during the Dry", he faces its seventy-five-mile dry stage, sitting loosely in the saddle, with the same cheery "So long, chaps".

Five miles to "get a pace up"—a drink and then that seventy-five miles of Dry, with any "temperature they can spare from other parts", and not one drop of water in all its length for the horses. Straight on top of that, with the same horses and the same temperature, a run of twenty miles, mails dropped at Newcastle Waters, and another run of fifty into Powell's Creek, dry or otherwise according to circumstances.

"Takes a bit of fizzing to get into the Powell before the fourth sun-down," the Fizzer says—for, forgetting that there can be no change of horses, and leaving no time for a "Spell" after the "seventy-five-mile dry", the time limit for that one hundred and fifty miles, in a country where four miles an hour is good travelling on good roads, has been fixed at three and a half days. "Four, they call it," said the Fizzer, "forgetting I can't leave the water till midday. Takes a bit of fizzing all right." And yet at Powell's Creek no one has yet discovered whether the Fizzer comes at sun-down, or the sun goes down when the Fizzer comes.

MRS AENEAS GUNN
FROM *WE OF THE NEVER-NEVER*

"The Pioneer", a postcard by J. Hutchings published by the New South Wales Bookstall Co. in their "Art Series". Little is known about the artist who contributed many similar scenes to this series (see also p. 3). The romantic themes he chose were as popular eighty years ago as they are among collectors today.

H

The Barbarous Mail-coach

On the whole, I may say I have seen the public carriages of a good many countries, some of them not very far advanced in civilisation; but in discomfort, insecurity, unpunctuality, and general barbarism, the mail between Bathurst and Sydney far surpasses them all. It professed in Sydney to arrive at Bathurst at six P.M., i.e. twenty-five hours and a half from Sydney. But we "knocked up" on the road (every second day, at least, they either "knock up" or "break down") and the passengers had to walk four miles to the next stage, from whence we sent back fresh horses to the mail. The result of this, and of some minor accidents, was, that we were four hours late, and did not get to Bathurst till ten.

John Robert Godley

Telephone:

Telephone:

Telephone:

Telephone:

Telephone:

Telephone:

H

Telephone:

Telephone:

Telephone:

Telephone:

Telephone:

Telephone:

H

OVERLAND FROM SYDNEY

A Young Doctor happens to meet with a Nurse he has known in one of the hospitals during the small-pox scare. The conversation of the Doctor causes a sensation with the other occupants of the carriage. From *Comicalities* by the Australian Press Agencies published in 1883.

I J

Telephone:

The G.P.O. Sydney, NSW. A postcard by A. H. Fullwood.

Telephone:

Telephone:

Telephone:

Telephone:

Telephone:

Telephone:

Telephone:

Telephone:

Telephone:

Telephone:

Telephone:

I J

Neither snow, nor rain, nor heat, nor gloom of night stays these couriers from the swift completion of their appointed rounds.

HERODOTUS, *HISTORY*

Herodotus is writing of the mounted couriers of Xerxes, but the sentence has been very fittingly inscribed on the facade of the New York City post office and could justly apply to the couriers of Australia Post as shown in this turn of the century postcard.

K

"I Give Fair Warning"
—An Infamous Correspondent

Dear Sir,

I wish to acquaint you with some of the occurrences of the present past and future.

In or about the spring of 1870 the ground was very soft a hawker named Mr Gould got his waggon bogged between Greta and my mother's house on the eleven mile creek.

I give fair warning to all those who has reason to fear me to sell out and give £10 out of every hundred towards the widow and orphan fund and do not attempt to reside in Victoria but as short a time as possible after reading this notice, neglect this and abide by the consequences, which shall be worse than the rust in the wheat in Victoria or the druth of a dry season to the grasshoppers in New South Wales I do not wish to give the order full force without giving timely warning, but I am a widows son outlawed and my orders *must be obeyed.*

Edward Kelly
from *The Jerilderie Letter*

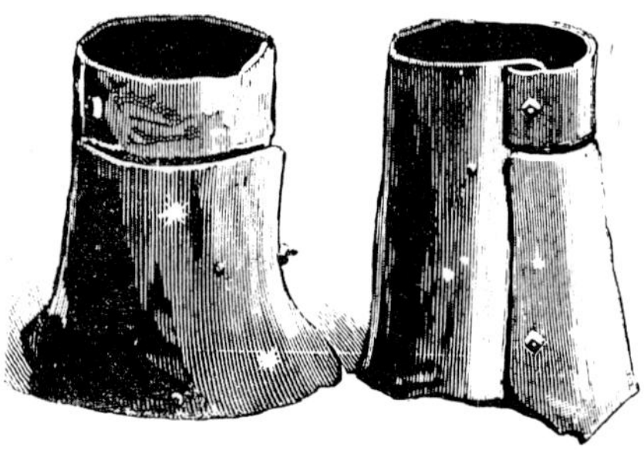

Telephone:

Telephone:

Telephone:

Telephone:

Telephone:

Telephone:

K

Telephone:

Telephone:

Telephone:

Telephone:

Telephone:

Telephone:

K

"STEAM COMMUNICATION"

A public meeting was held in Sydney, to consider the question of steam communication between Sydney and England. A committee was appointed to collect information on the subject, and the result was the recommendation of a postal service between this colony and England, which was subsequently adopted by a Committee of the Legislature. The route by way of Singapore was adopted. At this time the latest intelligence from England was generally five months old.

Intelligence first received that the Lords of the Admiralty had advertised for tenders for the conveyance of the mails between Sydney and Singapore, January 15, 1849. The colonists were without the mails which were despatched from London on the 1st September, in the previous year. During this year the contract for the conveyance of mails was entered into by way of Singapore and Torres Straits, with the Indian and Australian Steam Packet Company. January, 1849.

The Government brought forward a measure for the introduction of a uniform rate of postage, 1849.

"Chusan", first steamer from England, arrived at Melbourne, June 23; arrived at Sydney, August 3, 1852.

A measure was passed in the Legislative Council for a reduction of charge for books sent by post. It was intended to foster a taste for literature and disseminate useful information throughout the colony, 1852.

The New South Wales Government offered a bonus varying from £6,000 to £20,000 for the establishment of a monthly line of steamers to England, 1852.

From J. H. Heaton's
A DICTIONARY OF DATES, 1879

L

This Prim Little Note

A minute later he sat down at the table again. An idea had occurred to him: he would write Polly a letter—a letter that called for acknowledgement—and form an opinion of the girl from her reply . . .

. . . he went out to the post with it himself. In one hand he carried the letter, in the other the candle-end stuck in a bottle that was known as a "Ballarat lantern"; for it was a pitch-dark night.

Trade was slack; in consequence he found the four days that had to pass before he could hope for an answer exceptionally long. After their lapse, he twice spent an hour at the Post Office, in a fruitless attempt to get near the little window. On returning from the second of these absences, he found the letter waiting for him; it had been delivered by hand.

So far good: Polly had risen to his fly! He broke the seal.

. . . Mahony read, smiled and laid the letter down—only to pick it up again. It pleased him, did this prim little note: there was just the right shade of formal reserve about it. Then he began to study particulars: grammar and spelling were correct; the penmanship was in the Italian style, minute, yet flowing, the letters dowered with generous loops and tails.

HENRY HANDEL RICHARDSON
FROM *THE FORTUNES OF RICHARD MAHONY*

Telephone:

Telephone:

Telephone:

Telephone:

Telephone:

Telephone:

L

L

Telephone:

Telephone:

Telephone:

Telephone:

Telephone:

Telephone:

The Arrival of the Post, a watercolour by B. Warwick.

Directions for Writing Calligraphy

1. The Writing paper should be parallel to the edge of the desk, and the left edge of the page on which you are writing should be opposite the middle of your chest.

2. Keep the body nearly erect (i.e., inclining slightly forward) almost square to the desk, an inch or two from it; place the feet a little apart firmly on the floor, with the knee directly over the instep.

3. Place the left hand (open) on the edge of the writing paper, the elbow near the side of the body, the fingers above and the thumb below the line to be written. The left arm should be placed only so far on the desk as to allow the left hand to steady the paper.

4. The right forearm above the wrist (but not the wrist) should rest on the desk. The forearm and the third and fourth fingers of the right hand should be the only parts to touch the desk.

5. The penholder should cross the forefinger just in front of the knuckle and at the beginning of a line should point towards the right shoulder. The forefinger should be placed on the top of the penholder, an inch from the point of the pen, and the second finger at the side. The pen should be lightly held, and the thumb and the first and second fingers should be but slightly bent.

6. In writing a line the whole forearm should move from the body, and be kept at right angles to the edge of the desk.

7. Care should be taken that the two points of the nib touch the paper evenly.

The secret of this script lies in
1. The slope which must be kept the same throughout the line,
2. The close, even spacing of the letters,
3. The contrasting thick and thins which must join smoothly.

FORMAL "COPPERPLATE" SCRIPT

Before drawing the capitals, practise these curves until you can do them in one stroke with an easy flowing movement.

A B C D E F G H I

J K L M N O P Q R

S T U V W X Y Z

These capitals are adaptable to the space available; e.g. this ... or this ... this ... or this.

Curves must be graceful and flowing, no angles.

a b c d e f f g h i j k l

* The length of Ascenders and Descenders should balance with the body.

m n o p p q r r s t u v

w x y z uan

Note - the Turns are never sharp or angular but rounded smoothly into the hairlines. Connecting hairlines flow upward and into the next letter about ½ way this point to be maintained throughout the line, as is also the close, even spacing between the letters.

M

Telephone:

Telephone:

Telephone:

Telephone:

Telephone:

Telephone:

Telephone:

Telephone:

Telephone:

Telephone:

Telephone:

Telephone:

M

Two of the charming series of postcards designed by May Gibbs and featuring her unique Gumnut babies. These cards have become valued collectors' items.

M

Telephone:

Telephone:

Telephone:

Telephone:

Telephone:

Telephone:

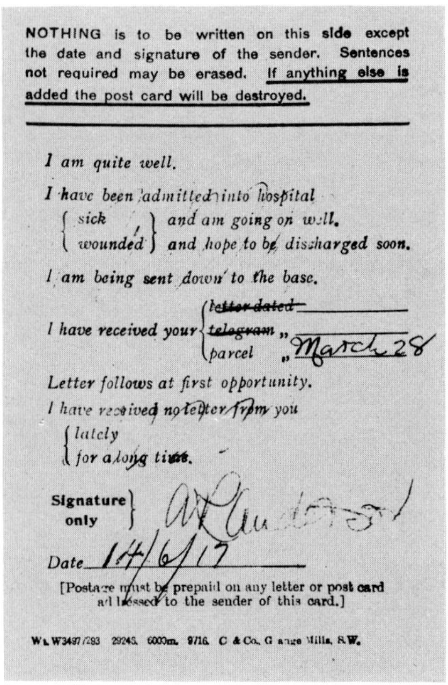

NOTHING is to be written on this side except the date and signature of the sender. Sentences not required may be erased. If anything else is added the post card will be destroyed.

I am quite well.

I have been admitted into hospital

sick / *wounded* } *and am going on well.* / *and hope to be discharged soon.*

I am being sent down to the base.

I have received your { ~~*letter dated*~~ / ~~*telegram*~~ „ / *parcel* „ March 28

Letter follows at first opportunity.

I have received no letter from you

{ *lately* / *for a long time.*

Signature only }

Date 14/6/17

[Postage must be prepaid on any letter or post card addressed to the sender of this card.]

W. W3497/293 29245. 6000m. 9/16. C & Co. Grange Mills, S.W.

Army letter card, 1915. Strike out some lines, sign and prepay the postage.

M

N

Telephone:

Telephone:

Telephone:

Telephone:

Telephone:

Telephone:

AIR MAIL — PALESTINE

"Praise God, from whom all blessings flow,"
The Padre said; and row on row
The rustling hymn books, in the sun,
Flickered, were folded. Then as one
A thousand voices stirred the air—
Were silent. Heads were bent in prayer.

Above the Padre's voice we heard
An engine drone; then, like a bird
With silvered wings, we saw the plane
Above the sandhills, out to sea,
Heading, with mail, to Galilee.

And in the clouds we saw again
Our homes; the noonday shimmering sun
On farm, and beach, and station run;
The stock knee-high in summer grass,
The shearers nodding as we pass
Each stand; the silos crammed with wheat,
The sheepdogs panting in the heat;
The breakers' curl, the lash of foam.
The aching, taunting thoughts of home.

"Praise God, from whom . . .", and each man bends
His head, to thank his God who sends
Halfway across the world, the mail:
Who deems those engines shall not fail,
But that they bring across the sea
The mail, to His own Galilee.

DAVID MCNICOLL

N

The Postman

I'd like to be a postman, and walk along the street,
Calling out, "Good Morning, Sir," to
gentlemen I meet,
Ringing every door-bell all along my beat,
In my cap and uniform so very nice and neat.
Perhaps I'd have a parasol in case of rain or heat;
But I wouldn't be a postman if . . .
The walking hurt my feet.
Would you?

C. J. Dennis

NEW·SOUTH·WALES·SYDNEY

Telephone:

Telephone:

Telephone:

Telephone:

Telephone:

Telephone:

N

O

Telephone:

Telephone:

Telephone:

Telephone:

Telephone:

Telephone:

A postcard from a series depicting Australian life.

P

Telephone:

Telephone:

Telephone:

Telephone:

Telephone:

Telephone:

To Remove Ink Stains

Ink Spots can be taken out of paper by the application of blotting paper which has been prepared by soaking in a solution of oxalic acid or oxalate of potassium.

Those who write much should always have a piece of this prepared blotting paper, for drying up blots made on letters or M.S.S.

MRS LANCE RAWSON
FROM *THE COLONIAL ENQUIRY BOOK*

P

Telephone:

Telephone:

Telephone:

Telephone:

Telephone:

Telephone:

P

The Travelling Post Office

The roving breezes come and go, the reed beds sweep and sway,
The sleepy river murmurs low, and loiters on its way,
It is the land of lots o' time along the Castlereagh.

The old man's son had left the farm, he found it dull and slow,
He drifted to the great North-west where all the rovers go.
"He's gone so long," the old man said, "he's dropped right out of mind,
But if you'd write a line to him I'd take it very kind;
He's shearing here and fencing there, a kind of waif and stray,
He's droving now with Conroy's sheep along the Castlereagh.

The sheep are travelling for the grass, and travelling very slow;
They may be at Mundooran now, or past the Overflow,
Or tramping down the black soil flats across by Waddiwong,
But all those little country towns would send the letter wrong,
The mailman, if he's extra tired, would pass them in his sleep,
It's safest to address the note to 'Care of Conroy's sheep',
For five and twenty thousand head can scarcely go astray,
You write to 'Care of Conroy's sheep along the Castlereagh'."

And now by coach and mailman's bag it goes from town to town,
And Conroy's Gap and Conroy's Creek have marked it "further down".
Beneath a sky of deepest blue where never cloud abides,

Telephone:

Telephone:

Telephone:

Telephone:

Telephone:

Telephone:

Telephone:

Telephone:

Telephone:

Telephone:

Telephone:

Telephone:

Q

A speck upon the waste of plain the lonely mailman
rides.
Where fierce hot winds have set the pine and myall
boughs asweep
He hails the shearers passing by for news of
Conroy's sheep.
By big lagoons where wildfowl play and crested
pigeons flock,
By campfires where the drovers ride around their
restless stock,
And past the teamster toiling down to fetch the
wool away
My letter chases Conroy's sheep along the
Castlereagh.

A. B. PATERSON

"Skin Hunters", a postcard by A. MacInnes published early this century.

R

Impassioned Correspondents

My Darling Florence,

I love you and am determined to make you mine so take heed. I will wait until eight o'clock under the lamp nearest to your house on Wednesday eve. If you are not there by that hour I will immediately seek an interview with your parents, and if they refuse to allow me to see you then I will force an entrance into your room, for see you I will, I swear it, if not by fair means then by foul.

Your desperate lover

Telephone:

Telephone:

Telephone:

Telephone:

Telephone:

Telephone:

R

Telephone:

Telephone:

Telephone:

Telephone:

Telephone:

Telephone:

Postcard messages from a bygone era.

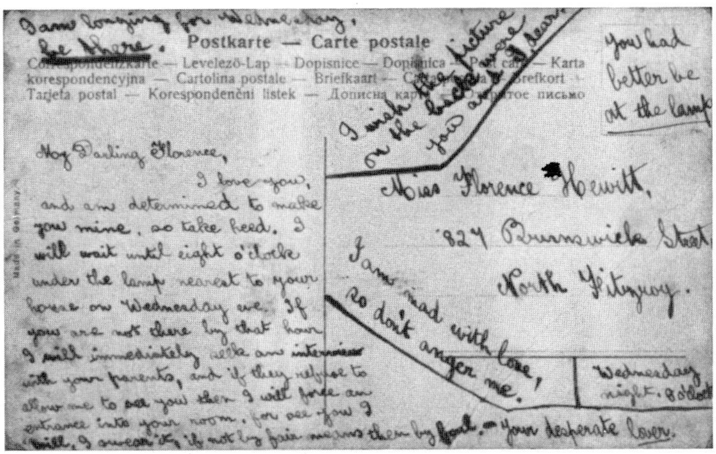

S

The Language of Flowers

The language of flowers has been called the language of refined and modest courtship. In days gone by many a secret message was conveyed by pressing a flower and enclosing it with a letter or proffering it when to utter the sentiment it conveyed would have been impossible. The following is a far from complete list but allows for a modest range of sentiments to be conveyed by a modern correspondent.

ABOVE: *Grevillea speciosa* by Adam Foster.

OPPOSITE: *Native Wildflowers* by Louisa Ann Meredith who was influential in popularising a sentimental interest in the language of flowers.

Telephone:

Telephone:

Telephone:

Telephone:

Telephone:

Telephone:

S

Acacia, Friendship
Acacia, Yellow, Secret Love
Acanthus, The Fine Arts
Acalia, Temperance
Almond, Hope
Allspice, Compassion
Aloe, Affliction
Amethyst, Admiration
Andromeda, Self-sacrifice
Anemone (Garden), Forsaken
Azalea, Temperance

Balsam, Impatience
Barberry, Sharpness of Temper
Basil, Hatred
Bluebell, Sorrowful Regret
Borage, Bluntness
Bur, You Weary Me
Buttercup, Childishness

Camellia, Red, Excellence
Camellia, White, Loveliness
Camomile, Energy in Adversity
Carnation, Striped, Refusal
Carnation, Deep Red, Poor Me
Candytuft, Indifference
Chrysanthemum, Red, I Love
Chrysanthemum, White, Truth
Chrysanthemum, Yellow, Slighted Love
Cineraria, Always Delightful
Cyclamen, Diffidence
Cypress, Death

Daffodil, Regard
Dahlia, Instability
Daisy, Innocence
Daisy, Michaelmas, Farewell

Forget-me-not, Forget-me-not
Foxglove, Insincerity

Gardenia, Refinement
Geranium, Dark, Melancholy
Horse-shoe Leaf, Stupiditiy
Ivy, Bridal Favour
Lemon, Unexpected Meeting
Nutmeg, Expected Meeting
Oak-leaved, True Friendship
Variegated, Ingenuity
Rose-scented, Preference
Scarlet, Comforting, Kindness
Silver-leaved, Recall
Wild, Steadfast Piety
Gladioli, Ready Armed

Heath, Solitude
Heliotrope, I Turn to Thee
Hellebore, Scandal
Hibiscus, Delicate Beauty
Holly, Foresight
Hollyhock, Fecundity

Lavender, Distrust
Lemon, Zest
Lily, White, Purity
Lily, Yellow, Falsehood

Marigold, Grief, Chagrin
French, Jealousy
and Cypress, Despair
Marjoram, Blushes

Oats, Harmony
Oleander, Beware
Olive, Peace
Orange Blossoms, Purity

Palm, Victory
Pansy, I Think of You
Parsley, Festivity, Feasting
Passion Flower, Superstition
Peach Blossom, Your Captive
Pear, Affection
Phlox, Unanimity

Ranunculus, Are Charming
Rose, Love
Rosemary, You Ever Revive
Rue, Scorn, Despite

Salvia, Blue, Wisdom
Salvia, Red, Energy
Saxifrage, Mossy, Affection
Snapdragon, "No."
Snowball, Bound
Snowdrop, Hope

Tamarisk, Crime
Tansy, I War Against You

Verbena, Pink, Family Union
Purple, I Weep for You
Scarlet, Unite Against Evil
Sweet-scented, Sensibility
White, Pray for Me

Wall-flower, Fidelity
Water Lily, Purity of Heart

S

For Posterity

In my early years, I never bothered to preserve any letters save those of Hugh McCrae, which were so delightful and enlivened with his little pen drawings as to be minor works of art. I certainly never expected anyone to preserve my scrawls, and it came as a shock to me when Bert Stevens died, and old George Robertson bought his letters; with mine among them. When I heard that G.R. was negotiating for them I wrote to Mrs Stevens, saying that I would pay her double the price of any offers for my letters. I knew there was so much intemperate stuff in them about people that I intended to burn them, but she sold them to G.R. This discovery that my letters, or letters in general, had a market value for collectors of Australiana so alarmed me that I ceased writing letters for a number of years; other than those dealing with business matters.

It took me some time to realize that burning letters—which may reveal to posterity the indiscreet procedure of one's private life—was simply fatuous. Everything becomes known about the life of one who has made a notable, or notorious, figure in his time.

YOURS EVER
Norman

EXTRACT FROM A LETTER
FROM NORMAN LINDSAY

Telephone:

Telephone:

Telephone:

Telephone:

Telephone:

Telephone:

S

Telephone:

Telephone:

Telephone:

Telephone:

Telephone:

Telephone:

S

The versatile and prolific Norman Lindsay also contributed to the series of humorous postcards published by the *Bulletin*. This one, from Bulletin Series III is, like all Lindsay's cards, much sought after by collectors.

T

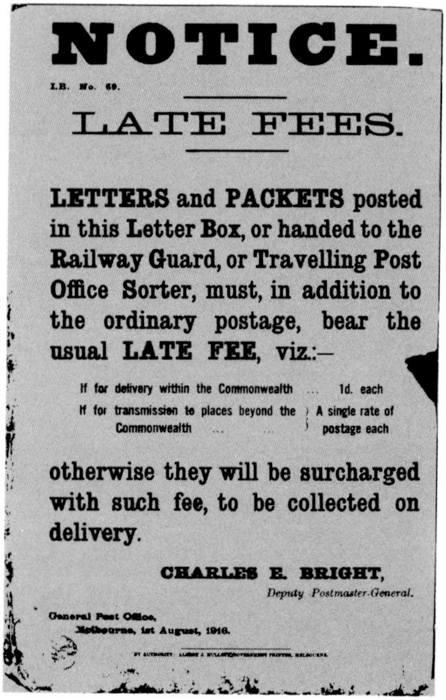

NOTICE.

I.B. No. 69.

LATE FEES.

LETTERS and **PACKETS** posted in this **Letter Box**, or handed to the **Railway Guard**, or **Travelling Post Office Sorter**, must, in addition to the ordinary postage, bear the usual **LATE FEE**, viz.:—

If for delivery within the Commonwealth ...	1d. each
If for transmission to places beyond the Commonwealth	A single rate of postage each

otherwise they will be surcharged with such fee, to be collected on delivery.

CHARLES E. BRIGHT,
Deputy Postmaster-General.

General Post Office,
Melbourne, 1st August, 1916.

Telephone:

Telephone:

Telephone:

Telephone:

Telephone:

Telephone:

T

Telephone:

Telephone:

Telephone:

Telephone:

Telephone:

Telephone:

T

Parcel Post Blokes

Round two o'clock the coach topped a low rise and seven miles onward could be seen the line of great red-gums bordering the Darling, and, amid the pepper trees, the shining roofs of Wilcannia.

. . . It was the priest who asked the meaning of "Parcels Post bloke".

"Well, your Reverence, the city offices of the Pastoral Companies seem to think that the back country wants new blood," explained the driver. "Like Arthur here, they send up young fellers, paying their fares if they stop a year. They get landed at the stations with the mail, sort of."

"Does the new blood upset the old?" pressed the priest . . .

"There's all sorts out in these parts. A lot of 'em were Parcels Post blokes themselves, blokes that I brought out from the Hill years ago. A lot of old coves, too, often go broke in Adelaide and get themselves sent up again by Parcels Post."

JESSICA HAWKE

FROM *FOLLOW MY DUST*
—A BIOGRAPHY OF ARTHUR UPFIELD

UV

LETTERS FORMAL

While a formal response to a formal invitation is still quite often used, other conventions in force in Victorian times have today given way to freer forms of expression. Some examples are given.

Starting and finishing a letter

When the salutation in a letter is "Dear Sir" or "Dear Madam" it is still correct to end it "Yours faithfully".

When addressing someone by name ("Dear Mr . . ."), "Yours sincerely" or "Yours truly" are the correct ways to end the letter.

Abbreviations

ult. (ultimo mense)—last month
inst. (instant)—this month
prox. (proxima mense)—next month
(all expressions to be deplored in modern usage)
R.S.V.P. (respondez s'il vous plait)—please reply
p.p. (per procurationem)—by proxy or for and on behalf of

Telephone:

Telephone:

Telephone:

Telephone:

Telephone:

Telephone:

Telephone:

Telephone:

Telephone:

Telephone:

Telephone:

Telephone:

UV

Formal Invitations

Mr and Mrs Benjimen Brandysnap
request the pleasure of the company of

Miss Mabel Spriggs

at the marriage of their daughter

Obelia
with
Mr Robert David Duckworth

at St Trinian's Parish Church, Toorak
on Saturday, 23 June 19.. at 11 a.m.
and afterwards at "Rosemount", South Yarra

14 Movington Close
South Yarra

R.S.V.P.

Mr and Mrs Roger Fortescue
request the pleasure of
Mr and Mrs Reginald Roberts' company
on Friday 18 September, 19.. at 7.00 p.m.

COCKTAILS

Knees-Up Downs
Monaro

R.S.V.P.

W

Telephone:

Telephone:

Telephone:

Telephone:

Telephone:

Telephone:

Formal Responses

Miss Mabel Spriggs thanks Mr and Mrs Benjimen Brandysnap for their kind invitation to the marriage of their daughter Obelia at St Trinian's Parish Church on Saturday 23 June, and has great pleasure in accepting (or)
and much regrets that she will be unable to attend as she will be out of the country on that date.

Mr and Mrs Reginald Roberts have much pleasure in accepting Mr and Mrs Roger Fortescue's kind invitation to cocktails on Friday 18 September at 7.00 p.m.

or

Mr and Mrs Reginald Roberts thank Mr and Mrs Roger Fortescue for the kind invitation to cocktails on Friday 18 September but regret they are unable to accept as they have a prior engagement.

Less Formal Responses

Thank you so much for your kind invitation to Obelia's wedding on 23 June. I would so much like to be there but am sorry to say that it coincides with a long-planned overseas trip. Please give her and Robert my love and best wishes and tell them that I shall be thinking of them. A small gift is on its way to them which I hope they will find useful in their new home.

Thank you both very much for your kind invitation to cocktails next Friday evening (the 18th) at 7 o'clock. Reg and I should both love to come and are looking forward to seeing you both again.

Telephone:

Telephone:

Telephone:

Telephone:

Telephone:

Telephone:

W

The Letter of Condolence

Perhaps the most difficult of all letters to write, but on this Mrs Emily Post gives excellent guidance.

"Intimate letters of condolence are like love letters in that they are too sacred to follow a set form. One rule, and one only, should guide you in writing such letters. Say what you truly feel. Say that and nothing else. Sit down at your desk; let your thoughts dwell on the person you are writing to. The more nearly a note can express a handclasp, a thought of sympathy, above all, a genuine love or appreciation of the one who has gone, the greater comfort it brings."

That having been said, the following are included merely as suggestive guides for those at a loss to construct an appropriate message.

MY DEAR . . .

We are so very much shocked to hear of the sorrow that has come to you.

If there is anything that either I or my husband can do, I earnestly hope that you will ask someone to call upon us.

. . . . . .

MY DEAR . . .

I know how little words written on a page can possibly mean to you at such a time. But I must at least tell you that you are in our thoughts and in our hearts, and if there is *anything* that we can do for you, please send us a message—whatever it may be.

WITH DEEPEST SYMPATHY,

. . . . . .

XYZ

Telephone:

Telephone:

Telephone:

Telephone:

Telephone:

Telephone:

The First Airmail Service

The first official airmail service from Australia to the UK was inaugurated in Melbourne on 23 April 1931. Mail originating in the southern States was flown from Melbourne to Sydney, where it was transferred to another aircraft holding New South Wales and New Zealand mail. (The New Zealand mail had been shipped to Sydney.) The mail was then flown to Brisbane where it was loaded onto the Qantas aircraft "Apollo" which contained the Queensland mail. The "Apollo" left for Darwin on 25 April 1931 on the last Australian leg of the airmail flight.

At Darwin, twenty-five mail bags weighing about 300 kg were loaded onto Kingsford Smith's aircraft "The Southern Cross", and on 27 April 1931 Kingsford Smith left Darwin for Burma. The mail bags were then transferred to an Imperial Airways aircraft, "City of Karachi", which left for Karachi on the same day. On arrival at Karachi, on 6 May 1931, the mail bags were consigned to the regular Imperial Airways Karachi to London mail plane. The plane arrived in England on 14 May 1931.

XYZ

Telephone:

Telephone:

Telephone:

Telephone:

Telephone:

Telephone:

Stamps issued to commemorate the first official airmail service between Australia and New Guinea.

The Kingsford Smith World Flights' stamp issued in time for use on mail carried on the first mail plane to England.

XYZ

Telephone:

Telephone:

Telephone:

Telephone:

Telephone:

Telephone:

POSTCODES*

A

A1 Mine Settlement 3723
Abbotsford (NSW) 2046
Abbotsford (VIC) 3067
Abbotsham 7315
Abercorn 4628
Aberdare 2325
Aberdeen (NSW) 2336
Aberdeen (TAS) 7310
Aberfeldie 3040
Aberfeldy (Moe) 3825
Aberfoyle Park 5159
Abermain 2326
Abernethy 2325
Acacia Plateau 2476
Acacia Ridge 4110
Acheron 3714
Acland 4352
Acton 7170
Acton (ACT) 2601
Adaminaby 2630
Adamstown 2289
Adavale 4474
Addington 3352
Addison Road 2204
ADELAIDE
CITY 5000
GPO PRIVATE BOXES 5001
Adelaide Airport 5000
Adelaide River (NT) 5783
Adelaide University 5000
Adelong 2729
Adjungbilly 2727
Advancetown 4211
Adventure Bay 7160
Adwill Place 2113
Aeroglen 4870
Agnes 3962
Agnew 6435
Ainslie (ACT) 2602
Airds 2560
Aireys Inlet 3221
Airlie Beach 4802
Airport West 3042
Aitkenvale 4814
Ajana 6532
Alawa (NT) 5792
Alawoona 5311
Albanvale 3021
Albany 6330
Albany Creek 4035
Albert 2873
Albert Park (SA) 5014
Albert Park (VIC) 3206
Alberton 4207
Alberton (SA) 5014
Alberton (TAS) 7254
Alberton (VIC) 3971
Albion (QLD) 4010
Albion (VIC) 3020
Albion Park 2527
Albury 2640
Alcomie 7330
Alderley (QLD) 4051
Aldersyde 6306
Aldgate 5154
Aldinga 5173
Alectown 2870
Alexandra (VIC) 3714
Alexandra Bridge 6288
Alexandra Headland 4572
Alexandra Hills 4161
Alexandria (NSW) 2015
Alford 5555
Alfords Point 2234
Alfred Cove 6154
Alfredton 3350
Algester 4115
Alice Springs 5750
Alice Springs (Community And Private Bags) 5751
Alinjarra 6064
Alkimos 6033
Allambie (NSW) 2100
Allans Flat 3691
Allansford 3277
Allanson 6225
Allawah 2218
Allenby Gardens 5009
Allendale 3364
Allendale East 5291
Allens Rivulet 7104
Allenstown 4700
Allestree 3306
Allingham 4850
Allora 4362
Allworth 2425
Allynbrook 2311
Alma 5401
Almaden 4871
Almurta 3979
Alonnah 7159
Aloomba 4871
Alpha 4724
Alphington 3078
Alstonville 2477
Altona 3018
Altona East 3025
Altona Gate 3025
Altona Meadows 3028
Altona North 3025
Alvie 3249
Alyangula 5798
Amamoor 4570
Ambarvale 2560
Amberley 4306
Amby 4462
Amelup 6338
American River 5221
Amiens 4352
Amity Point 4183
Amphitheatre 3468
Anakie (QLD) 4702
Anakie (VIC) 3221
Ancona 3715
Andamooka Opal Fields 5722
Andergrove 4740
Anderson 3995
Ando 2631
Andover 7120
Andrews 4220
Angaston 5353
Angellala 4455
Angle Park 5010
Angle Vale 5117
Anglers Paradise 4216
Anglers Rest 3898
Anglesea 3230
Anglesea Barracks 7002
Angurugu 5791
Anketell 6167
Anna Bay 2301
Annandale 2038
Annangrove 2156
Annerley 4103
Annuello 3549
Ansons Bay 7216
Anstead 4070
Antill Ponds 7120
Antwerp 3422
Anula (NT) 5793
Apollo Bay 3233
Appila 5480
Appin (NSW) 2560
Appin (VIC) 3578
Appin Park 3677
Applecross 6153
Applethorpe 4378
Apslawn 7190
Apsley 7030
Apsley (VIC) 3319
Araluen (NSW) 2622
Aramac 4726
Arana Hills 4054
Aranda (ACT) 2614
Ararat 3377
Aratula 4309
Arcadia (NSW) 2159
Arcadia (VIC) 3613
Arcadia Bay 4816
Arcadia Vale 2283
Archerfield 4108
Archerton 3723
Archies Creek 3992
Ardath 6419
Ardeer 3022
Ardglen 2338
Ardlethan 2665
Ardmona 3629
Ardross 6153
Ardrossan 5571
Areegra 3480
Argenton 2284
Argents Hill 2449
Argyle (WA) 6239
Ariah Park 2665
Arkona 3414
Armadale (VIC) 3143
Armadale (WA) 6112
Armatree 2831
Armidale (NSW) 2350
Arncliffe 2205
Arno Bay 5603
Arnold 3551
Arrino 6519
Artarmon 2064
Arthur River (TAS) 7330
Arthur River (WA) 6315
Arthurs Creek 3099
Arthurton 5572
Arthurville 2820
Ascot (QLD) 4007
Ascot (VIC) 3364
Ascot Park 5043
Ascot Vale 3032
Ashbourne (SA) 5157
Ashbourne (VIC) 3442
Ashburton 3147
Ashbury 2193
Ashcroft 2168
Ashfield (NSW) 2131
Ashfield (WA) 6054
Ashford (NSW) 2361
Ashford (SA) 5035
Ashgrove 4060
Ashley (NSW) 2400
Ashmore 4214
Ashton 5137
Ashwood Via Ashburton 3147
Ashwood Via Burwood 3125
Aspendale 3195
Aspley (QLD) 4034
Asquith 2078
Athelstone 5076
Atherton 4883
Athlone 3818
Athol Park 5012
Attadale 6156
Attunga 2345
Auburn 3123
Auburn (NSW) 2144
Auburn (SA) 5451
Auburn South 3122
Auchenflower 4066
Audley 2232
Augathella 4477
Augusta 6290
Auldana 5072
Aurukun 4871
Austinmer 2515
Austins Ferry 7011
Austral 2171
Australian Defence Forces (C/- IMC) 2890
Australian National University (ACT) 2601
Australind 6230
Avalon Beach 2107
Avenel 3664
Avenue Range 5273
Avoca (TAS) 7213
Avoca (VIC) 3467
Avoca Beach 2260
Avon 5501
Avon Plains 3478
Avondale (QLD) 4672
Avondale Heights 3034
Awaba 2283
Axedale 3551
Ayers Rock (NT) 5751
Aylmerton 2575
Ayr 4807
Ayrford 3268

B

Baan Baa 2383
Baandee 6412
Baarmutha 3747
Babakin 6428
Babinda 4861
Bacala 7254
Bacchus Marsh 3340
Back Creek 7252
Baddaginnie 3670
Baddow 4650
Baden 7120
Baden Powell 3199
Badgebup 6317
Badger Corner 7255
Badger Creek 3777
Badgerys Creek 2171
Badgingarra 6521
Baerami Creek 2333
Bagdad 7030
Bagnoo 2446
Bagot (NT) 5790
Bagshot 3551
Bahgallah 3312
Bahr's Scrub 4207
Baileston 3608
Bairnsdale 3875
Bajool 4699
Bakers Hill 6562
Bakers Swamp 2820
Bakewell (NT) 5786
Balaclava (VIC) 3183
Balaklava (SA) 5461
Balcatta 6021
Balcombe 3934
Bald Hills (QLD) 4036
Baldivis 6171
Baldry 2867
Balga 6061
Balgowlah 2093
Balgownie 2519
Balhannah 5242
Balingup 6253
Balladoran 2831
Ballajura 6066
Ballalaba 2622
Ballan 3342
Ballandean 4382
Ballarat 3350
Ballarat RSD 3352
Balldale 2646
Ballendella 3561
Ballengarra 2441
Balliang 3340
Ballidu 6606
Ballimore 2830
Ballina 2478
Balmain 2041
Balmattum 3666
Balmoral (QLD) 4171
Balmoral (Spit Junction - NSW) 2088
Balmoral (VIC) 3407
Balmoral Village 2571
Balnarring 3926
Balook 3971
Balranald 2715
Balwyn 3103
Balwyn East 3129
Balwyn West 3101
Bamaga 4876
Bamawm 3561
Bambra 3241
Banana 4702
Bandiana Mil. P.O. 3694
Bandongrove 2420
Bangalow 2479
Bangor (NSW) 2234
Bangor (TAS) 7254
Banjup 6164
Banksia 2216
Banksia Beach 4507
Banksia Park 5091
Banksiadale 6213
Banksmeadow 2019
Bankstown 2200
Bankstown East 2190
Bannerton 3549
Bannister (NSW) 2580
Bannister (WA) 6391
Bannockburn (QLD) 4207
Bannockburn (VIC) 3331
Banool 3249
Banora Point 2486
Banyena 3388
Banyo 4014
Banyule 3084
Bapaume 4352
Bar Beach 2300
Bar Point 2253
Baradine 2396
Baralaba 4702
Baranduda 3691
Barcaldine 4725
Bardon 4065
Bardouroka 2315
Bardwell Park 2207
Bare Island 2036

*Please note that postcode changes do occur. Consult a Post Office postcode book or your local telephone directory for the latest postcodes.

Bareena 3220
Barellan 2665
Barellan Point 4306
Bargara 4670
Bargo 2574
Barham 2739
Baring 3491
Baringhup 3463
Barjarg 3721
Barker Centre (ACT) 2603
Barkers Creek 3451
Barkly 3381
Barkstead 3364
Barmah Town 3639
Barmedman 2668
Barmera 5345
Barnadown 3557
Barnawartha 3688
Barnes Bay 7156
Barney Point 4680
Barneys Point 2486
Barnsley 2301
Barongarook 3249
Barooga (NSW) 3644
Barraba 2347
Barrack Heights 2528
Barrack Point 2528
Barragup 6210
Barramunga 3249
Barraport 3537
Barrengarry 2577
Barretta 7153
Barrington (NSW) 2422
Barrington (TAS) 7306
Barringun 2840
Barrow Creek 5751
Barrow Island 6712
Barry 2799
Barry Beach 3962
Bartle Freer 4861
Barton (ACT) 2600
Barwick 2372
Barwon Downs 3243
Barwon Heads 3227
Baryulgil 2460
Basin Pocket 4305
Basin View 2540
Baskerville 6056
Basket Range 5138
Bass 3991
Bass Hill 2197
Bassendean 6054
Batchelor 5791
Bateau Bay 2261
Batehaven 2536
Bateman 6155
Batemans Bay 2536
Bathurst 2795
Batlow 2730
Batman 3058
Battery Point 7000
Baulkham Hills 2153
Bauple 4650
Baxter 3911
Bayindeen 3375
Bayldon 2452
Bayles 3981
Baynton 3444
Bayswater (VIC) 3153
Bayswater (WA) 6053
Bayview (NSW) 2104
Beach Lands 6530
Beachmere 4510
Beachport 5280
Beacon 6472
Beacon Hill 2100
Beaconsfield (NSW) (PO And Private Boxes) 2014
Beaconsfield (NSW) (Street Addresses) 2015
Beaconsfield (TAS) 7251
Beaconsfield (VIC) 3807
Beaconsfield (WA) 6162
Beaconsfield Upper 3808
Bealiba 3475
Beardmores 3825
Bears Lagoon 3517
Beaudesert 4285
Beaufort 3373
Beaufort River 6395
Beaumaris 3193
Beaumont (NSW) 2577
Beaumont (SA) 5066
Beauty Point (Mosman - NSW) 2088
Beauty Point (TAS) 7251
Beazleys Bridge 3478
Becher 6172
Beckenham 6107
Beckom 2665
Bedford 6052
Bedford Park 5042
Bedfordale 6112
Bedgerebong 2871
Bedourie 4829
Beeac 3251
Beech Forest 3237
Beechboro 6063
Beechford 7252
Beechwood 2446
Beechworth 3747
Beecroft 2119
Beelbangera 2680
Beenleigh 4207
Beerburrum 4517
Beerwah 4519
Bega 2550
Bel Air (Adamstown) 2289
Belair (SA) 5052
Belbora 2422
Belconnen (ACT) (Private Boxes) 2616
Belconnen (ACT) (Street Addresses) 2617
Beldon 6025
Belfield 2191
Belford 2335
Belgian Gardens 4810
Belgrave 3160
Belhus 6055
Belka 6417
Bell 2786
Bell (QLD) 4408
Bell Bay 7253
Bell Park 3215
Bell Post Hill 3215
Bellamack (NT) 5786
Bellambi 2518
Bellangry 2446
Bellara 4507
Bellarine 3221
Bellata 2397
Bellbird 2325
Bellbird Creek 3889
Bellbird Park 4300
Bellbowrie 4070
Bellbrae Vic 3228
Bellbridge 3691
Bellbrook 2440
Bellenden Ker 4871
Bellerive 7018
Bellevue 6056
Bellevue Heights 5050
Bellevue Hill (NSW) 2023
Bellimbopinni 2440
Bellingen 2454
Belltrees 2337
Belmont (NSW) 2280
Belmont (QLD) 4153
Belmont (VIC) 3216
Belmont (WA) 6104
Belmore 2192
Belrose 2085
Beltana 5730
Bemboka 2550
Bemm River 3889
Ben Buckler 2026
Ben Lomond 2365
Bena 3946
Benalla 3672
Benambra 3900
Benandarah 2536
Benarby 4680
Benarch 3630
Benarkin 4306
Benayeo 3319
Bencubbin 6477
Bendalong 2539
Bendemeer 2352
Bendering 6367
Bendick Murrell 2803
Bendigo 3550
Bendoc 3888
Benerembah 2680
Benger 6223
Bengworden 3875
Beni 2830
Benjaberring 6463
Benjeroop 3579
Bennetts Green 2290
Bennetts Head 2428
Bennettswood Via Box Hill 3128
Bennettswood Via Burwood 3125
Bennison 3960
Benowa 4217
Bensville 2256
Bentleigh 3204
Bentley (NSW) 2480
Bentley (WA) 6102
Berajondo 4675
Berala 2141
Beremboke 3342
Beresfield 2322
Beresford 6530
Bergalia 2537
Berkeley 2506
Berkeley Vale 2259
Berkshire Park 2765
Bermagui 2547
Berowra 2081
Berowra Heights 2082
Berowra Waters 2082
Berri (SA) 5343
Berridale (NSW) 2628
Berriedale 7011
Berrigan 2712
Berrilee 2159
Berrima 2577
Berrimah 5788
Berrinba 4117
Berringa 3351
Berringama 3691
Berringer 2539
Berriwillock 3531
Berry (NSW) 2535
Berrybank 3323
Berrys Bay 2060
Berrys Creek 3953
Berwick 3806
Bessiebelle 3304
Bet Bet 3472
Bete Bolong 3888
Bethanga 3691
Bethania 4205
Bethungra 2590
Betley 3472
Beulah (TAS) 7306
Beulah (VIC) 3395
Beulah Park 5067
Beverford 3590
Beveridge 3753
Beverley (SA) 5009
Beverley (WA) 6304
Beverley Park 2217
Beverly Hills (NSW) 2209
Bexhill 2480
Bexley 2207
Bibbenluke 2632
Bibra Lake 6163
Bicheno 7215
Bickley 6076
Bicton 6157
Bidwell 2770
Big Pats Creek 3799
Bigga 2583
Biggara 3707
Biggenden 4621
Biggera Waters 4216
Biggs Flat (SA) 5153
Bilambil 2486
Bilbarin 6375
Bilbul 2680
Bilgola 2107
Bilinga 4225
Billimari 2804
Billinudgel 2483
Biloela 4715
Bilpin 2758
Bimbi 2810
Binalong 2584
Binalong Bay 7216
Binda 2583
Bindi (VIC) 3896
Bindi Bindi (WA) 6574
Bindoon 6502
Bingara 2404
Bingil Bay 4854
Binginwarri 3966
Bingo 3898
Biniguy 2394
Binna Burra 2479
Binnaway 2395
Binnu 6532
Binnum 5262
Binya 2665
Birchgrove 2041
Birchip 3483
Birchs Bay 7162
Birdsville 4482
Birdwood 5234
Birdwoodton 3505
Birkdale 4159
Birkenhead 5015
Birmingham Gardens 2287
Birralee 7303
Birregurra 3242
Birriwa 2844
Birrong 2143
Birtinya 4575
Bishops Bridge 2326
Bishopsbourne 7301
Bittern 3918
Black Forest 5035
Black Hill (SA) 5353
Black Hill (VIC) 3350
Black Hills 7140
Black Mountain (NSW) 2365
Black River 7321
Black Rock (SA) 5430
Black Rock (VIC) 3193
Black Springs (NSW) 2787
Black Swamp (NSW) 2372
Blackall 4472
Blackalls 2283
Blackburn 3130
Blackbutt (QLD) 4306
Blackett 2770
Blackheath (NSW) 2785
Blackmans Bay 7152
Blackmans Point 2444
Blacksmiths 2281
Blackstone 4304
Blacktown 2148
Blackville 2343
Blackwall (NSW) 2256
Blackwall (TAS) 7251
Blackwarry 3844
Blackwater 4717
Blackwood (SA) 5051
Blackwood (VIC) 3458
Blackwood Creek 7301
Blackwood RMD (SA) 5157
Blains 3564
Blair Athol (SA) 5084
Blairgowrie 3942
Blakehurst 2221
Blampied 3364
Blanchetown 5357
Blanchview 4352
Blandford 2338
Blanket Flat 2583
Blaxcell 2142
Blaxland 2774
Blayney 2799
Bleak House 3418
Blessington 7212
Blighty 2713
Blinman 5730
Bloomsbury 4799
Blowhard 3352
Blue Bay 2261
Blue Lagoon 2261
Blue Rocks 7255
Blues Point 2060
Bluewater 4816
Bluff 4702
Bluff Point 6530
Blyth 5462
Blythe Heads 7316
Boambee 2450
Boat Harbour (TAS) 7321
Bobadah 2877
Bobin 2429
Bobinawarrah 3678
Bobs Farm 2301
Bodalla 2545
Bodallin 6424
Bodangora 2820
Boddington 6390
Bogan Gate 2876
Bogangar 2488
Bogantungan Via Rockhampton 4702
Boggabilla 2409
Boggabri 2382
Bogong 3699
Bohle 4816
Bohnock 2430
Boho South 3669
Boigbeat 3531
Boinka 3490
Boisdale 3860
Bokarina 4575
Bolgart 6568
Bolinda 3432
Bolivar 5110
Bolivia 2372
Bollon 4488
Bolong 2540
Bolton 3546
Bolton Point 2283
Bolwarra (NSW) 2320
Bolwarrah (VIC) 3352
Bomaderry 2541
Bombala 2632
Bombo 2533
Bon Accord 2650
Bonalbo 2470
Bonang 3888
Bonavista 4800
Bonbeach Via Carrum 3197
Bonbeach Via Chelsea 3196
Bondi 2026
Bondi Junction 2022
Bonegilla (Roadside) 3691
Bonegilla Milpo 3693
Bongaree 4507
Bongeen 4356
Bonnells Bay 2264
Bonnet Bay 2226
Bonnet Hill 7006
Bonnie Brae 3960
Bonnie Doon 3720
Bonnie Rock 6479
Bonny Hills 2445
Bonnyrigg 2177
Bonogin 4213
Bonshaw 2361
Bonville 2441
Booborowie 5417
Boogan 4871
Booker Bay 2257
Bookham 2582
Boolambayte 2423
Boolarong 3960
Boolaroo 2284
Boolarra 3870
Booleroo Centre 5482
Booligal 2711
Boomi 2405
Boonah (QLD) 4310
Boondall 4034
Boonoo Boonoo 2372
Booragoon 6154
Booragul 2284
Booral 2425
Boorcan 3265
Boorhaman 3678
Boorhaman North 3685
Booroolite 3723
Booroorban 2710
Boorowa 2586
Boort 3537
Booval 4304
Borambil 2329
Borden 6338
Borderdale 6320
Bordertown 5268
Boree Creek 2652
Boreen Point 4565
Borenore 2800
Bornholm 6330
Boro 2622
Boronia 3155
Boronia Park 2111
Bororen 4678
Borrika 5309
Borroloola 5772
Borung 3535
Bossley Park 2176
Bostobrick 2453
Botany 2019
Bothwell 7030
Boulder 6432
Boulia 4829
Boundary Bend 3599
Bourke 2840
Bow 2329
Bow Bowing 2566
Bow Bridge 6333
Bow Hill 5238
Bowden 5007
Bowelling 6225
Bowen 4805
Bowen Hills 4006
Bowenfels 2790
Bowenvale 3465
Bowenville 4404
Bower 5374
Bowling Alley Point 2340
Bowmans 5550
Bowmans Forest 3735
Bowna 2644
Bowning 2582
Bowral 2576
Bowraville 2449
Box Hill (Riverstone - NSW) 2765

Box Hill (VIC) 3128
Box Hill North 3129
Boxwood 3725
Boya 6056
Boyanup 6237
Boydtown Park 2551
Boyer 7140
Boyup Brook 6244
Bracken Ridge 4017
Bracknell 7302
Bradbury (NSW) 2560
Bradbury (SA) 5153
Braddon (ACT) 2601
Bradfordville 2580
Bradys Marsh 7140
Braefield 2339
Braeside 3195
Brahma Lodge 5109
Braidwood 2622
Bramley 6285
Branditt 3630
Brandon 4808
Brandon Park 3170
Branxholm (TAS) 7254
Branxholme (VIC) 3302
Branxton 2335
Brassall 4305
Bray Park (NSW) 2484
Bray Park (QLD) 4500
Braybrook 3019
Breadalbane (NSW) 2581
Breadalbane (TAS) 7250
Breakfast Creek 4010
Breakwater 3219
Bream Creek 7175
Breamlea 3227
Bredbo 2626
Breeza 2381
Bremer 4305
Bremer Bay 6338
Brentwood (SA) 5575
Brentwood (WA) 6153
Breona 7304
Bretti 2422
Brewarrina 2839
Brewongle 2795
Briagolong 3860
Briar Hill 3088
Bribbaree 2594
Bribie Island 4507
Brickmakers Bay 7321
Bridgeman Downs 4035
Bridgenorth 7251
Bridgetown 6255
Bridgewater 7030
Bridgewater (SA) 5155
Bridgewater (VIC) 3516
Bridport 7254
Brigalow 4412
Briggsvale 2453
Bright 3741
Brighton 7030
Brighton (QLD) 4017
Brighton (SA) 5048
Brighton (VIC) 3186
Brighton Beach Via Brighton 3186
Brighton Beach Via Hampton 3188
Brighton East 3187
Brighton-Le-Sands (NSW) 2216
Brightwaters 2264
Brim 3391
Brindabella (ACT) 2611
Bringalbert 3319
Bringelly 2171
Brinkin (NT) 5792
Brinkworth 5464
BRISBANE
CITY 4000
GPO PRIVATE BOXES 4001
Brisbane Airport 4007
Brisbane Market 4106
Brisbane North Quay 4002
Brisbane Parliament House 4000
Brisbane Roma St 4003
Brit Brit 3315
Brittons Swamp 7330
Broad Arrow 6431
Broadbeach 4218
Broadford 3658
Broadmarsh 7030
Broadmeadow (NSW) 2292
Broadmeadows (VIC) 3047
Broadview 5083
Broadwater 3301
Broadwater (NSW) 2472
Broadway (NSW) 2007
Broadway (QLD) 4006
Broadway Nedlands 6009
Brocklehurst 2830
Brocklesby 2642
Brodies Plains 2360
Brodribb River 3889
Brogo 2550
Broke 2330
Broken Head 2481
Broken Hill 2880
Brompton 5007
Bronte 2024
Bronte Park 7140
Brookfield (QLD) 4069
Brookhampton 6239
Brooklea 3012
Brooklet (NSW) 2479
Brooklyn (NSW) 2253
Brooklyn (TAS) 7320
Brooklyn Park (SA) 5032
Brooklyn Via Altona North (VIC) 3025
Brooklyn Via Footscray West (VIC) 3012
Brookside Centre 4053
Brookstead 4352
Brookton 6306
Brookvale (NSW) 2100
Broome 6725
Broomehill 6318
Broomfield 3364
Brooms Head 2463
Brooweena 4620
Broulee 2537
Brown Hill 3350
Browns Creek 2799
Browns Plains (QLD) 4118
Browns Plains (VIC) 3685
Brownsville 2530
Bruarong 3749
Bruce (ACT) 2617
Bruce Rock 6418
Brukunga 5252
Brungle 2722
Brunkerville 2323
Brunswick 3056
Brunswick East 3057
Brunswick Heads 2483
Brunswick Junction 6224
Brunswick South 3055
Brunswick West 3055
Brush Creek 2259
Brushgrove 2460
Bruthen 3885
Buangor 3375
Bucasia 4750
Buccleuch 5301
Buchan 3885
Buckingham 6225
Buckland 7190
Buckleboo 5641
Buckley 3240
Buckrabanyule 3525
Buddina 4575
Buderim 4556
Budgewoi 2262
Buff Point 2262
Buffalo 3958
Buffalo River 3737
Bugaldie 2357
Builyan 4680
Bukkulla 2360
Bulahdelah 2423
Buldah 3889
Bulga (NSW) 2330
Bulgandry 2642
Bulgarra 6714
Bulgobac 7321
Bulimba 4171
Bulingary 2447
Bull Creek 6155
Bulla 3047
Bullaburra 2784
Bullaring 6373
Bullarook 3352
Bullarto 3461
Bulleen 3105
Bullengarook 3437
Bullfinch 6484
Bulli 2516
Bullsbrook 6084
Bullumwaal 3875
Buln Buln 3821
Bulyee 6306
Bumbaldry 2794
Bumberrah 3902
Bunaloo 2739
Bunbartha 3634
Bunbury 6230
Bundaberg 4670

Artist's impression of Brisbane's first Post Office 1839, formerly quarters of the Superintendent of Convicts. The Post Office occupied two units in the building on the right from about 1852 and 1872.

Bundalaguah 3851
Bundall 4217
Bundalong 3730
Bundamba 4304
Bundanoon 2578
Bundarra 2359
Bundeena 2230
Bunding 3342
Bundook 2422
Bundoora 3083
Bungador 3256
Bungalow 4870
Bungana 7254
Bungarby 2630
Bungaree (VIC) 3352
Bungeet 3726
Bungendore 2621
Bungonia 2580
Bungowannah 2642
Bungulla (NSW) 2372
Bungunya 4494
Bungwahl 2423
Buniche 6353
Buninyong 3357
Bunnan 2337
Buntine 6613
Bunya (QLD) 4055
Bunyah (NSW) 2429
Bunyan 2630
Bunyaville 4053
Bunyip 3815
Burakin 6467
Buranda 4102
Burbank 4156
Burcher 2671
Burekup 6227
Burges Siding 6302
Burgess Beach 2428
Burgooney 2669
Burketown 4830
Burleigh 3795
Burleigh Heads 4220
Burnbank 3371
Burnett Heads 4670
Burnie 7320
Burnley 3121
Burns 6028
Burns Creek 7212
Burnside (SA) 5066
Buronga 2648
Burpengary 4505
Burra 5417
Burra 2722
Burra Creek 2620
Burracoppin 6421
Burradoo 2576
Burraga 2795
Burragate 2550
Burraneer 2230
Burrawang 2577
Burrell Creek 2429
Burren Junction 2386
Burrill Lake 2539
Burringbar 2483
Burrinjuck 2582
Burroway 2821
Burrowye 3709
Burrum Heads 4659
Burrumbeet 3352
Burrumbuttock 2642
Burton 5110
Burwood (NSW) 2134
Burwood (VIC) 3125
Burwood East 3151
Burwood Heights (NSW) 2136
Burwood Heights (VIC) 3151
Busby 2168
Bushfield 3282
Bushy Park 7140
Busselton 6280
Butchers Ridge 3885
Bute 5560
Butler 6032
Butler Tanks 5605
Butlers Gorge 7140
Buxton (NSW) 2571
Buxton (VIC) 3711
Byabarra 2446
Byaduk 3301
Byaduk North 3300
Byford 6201
Bygalorie 2669
Bylands 3762
Bylong 2849
Byrneside 3617
Byrneville 3401
Byrock 2831
Byron Bay 2481

C

Cabarita (NSW) 2137
Cabarita (VIC) 3505
Cabarita Beach 2488
Cabarlah 4352
Cabbage Tree Creek 3889
Cabbage Tree Island 2477
Caboolture 4510
Cabramatta 2166
Cabramurra 2630
Cadell 5321
Cadoux 6466
Cairn Curran Reservoir 3463
Cairns 4870
Cairns Bay 7116
Cairns Forward 4871
Cairns Tableland Forward 4872
Cal Lal 2648
Calamvale 4116
Calca 5671
Calder 7325
Caldermeade 3984
Calen 4798
Calga 2250
California Gully 3556
Calingiri 6569
Calista 6167
Calivil 3573
Callala Bay 2540
Callala Beach 2540
Callawadda 3381
Callignee 3844
Callington 5254
Calliope (QLD) 4680
Caloundra 4551
Caltowie 5490
Calulu 3875
Calwell (ACT) 2905
Camberwell (NSW) 2330
Camberwell (VIC) 3124
Cambewarra 2540
Cambooya 4358
Cambrai 5353
Cambrian Hill 3352
Cambridge 7170
Cambridge Park 2750
Camdale 7320
Camden 2570
Camden Haven 2443
Camden Park (NSW) 2568
Camden Park (SA) 5038
Camellia 2142
Camena 7316
Camira 4300
Camira Creek 2470
Cammeray 2062
Camooweal 4828
Camp Hill 4152
Camp Mountain 4520
Campania 7026
Campbell (ACT) 2601
Campbell Town (TAS) 7210
Campbellfield 3061
Campbells Bridge 3381
Campbells Creek 3451
Campbells Forest 3556
Campbells Hill 2320
Campbelltown (NSW) 2560
Campbelltown (SA) 5074
Campbelltown (VIC) 3364
Camperdown (NSW) 2050
Camperdown (VIC) 3260
Campsie 2194
Canada Bay 2046
Canadian 3350
Canadian Bay 3930
Canal Estates 4217
Canbelego 2831
CANBERRA
CITY GPO (ACT) 2601
CITY GPO (ACT) PRIVATE BOXES 2601
Canberra Hospital (ACT) 2601
Canberra Parliament House (ACT) 2600
Canberra RAAF (ACT) 2600
Candelo 2550
Cangai 2461
Caniambo 3630
Canley Heights 2166
Canley Vale 2166
Cann River 3889
Canna 6627
Cannie 3540
Canning Bridge - Applecross 6153
Canning Mills 6111
Canning Vale 6155
Cannington 6107
Cannon Hill 4170
Cannons Creek 3977
Cannonvale 4802
Canowindra 2804
Canterbury (NSW) 2193
Canterbury (VIC) 3126
Canungra 4275
Capalaba 4157
Caparra 2429
Cape Barren Island 7257
Cape Bridgewater 3306
Cape Clear 3351
Cape Everard 3889
Cape Moreton 4025
Cape Otway 3233
Cape Paterson 3995
Cape Portland 7254
Cape Riche 6328
Cape Sorell 7468
Cape Woolamai 3925
Capeen 2470
Capel 6271
Capella 4702
Capertee 2846
Captains Flat 2621
Carabooda 6033
Carabost 2650
Caragabal 2810
Caramut 3274
Carapooee 3478
Carapook 3312
Carbarup 6324
Carboor 3678
Carbrook 4130
Carbunup River 6282
Carcoar 2791
Cardiff (NSW) 2285
Cardigan 3352
Cardinia 3978
Cardross 3496
Cardstone 4854
Cardup 6201
Cardwell 4816
Careel Bay 2107
Carey Bay 2283
Carey Gully 5144
Carey Park 6230
Cargo 2800
Carina (QLD) 4152
Carinda 2831
Carindale 4152
Carine 6020
Caringbah 2229
Carisbrook 3464
Carlingford 2118
Carlingford Shop Square 2118
Carlisle 6101
Carlisle River 3239
Carlotta 6275
Carlsruhe 3442
Carlsruhe Rail 3444
Carlton (NSW) 2218
Carlton (TAS) 7173
Carlton (VIC) 3053
Carmel 6076
Carmentown 7316
Carmila 4739
Carnamah 6517
Carnarvon 6701
Carnegie 3163
Carngham 3351
Caroda 2347
Carole Park (QLD) 4300
Caroling 6383
Carool 2486
Caroona 2343
Carpendeit 3256
Carpenter Rocks 5291
Carrajung 3844
Carrajung South 3874
Carramar 2163
Carranballac 3361
Carrara 4211
Carrathool 2711
Carrick (TAS) 7257
Carrieton 5432
Carrington 2294
Carroll 2340
Carrow Brook 2330
Carrum 3197
Carrum Downs 3201
Carseldine 4034
Carss Park 2221
Cartwright 2168
Carwarp 3494
Cascade (NSW) 2453
Casey (Antarctica) 7150
Cashmere 4500
Casino 2470
Cassillis (NSW) 2329
Castella 3777
Casterton 3311
Castle Cove 2069
Castle Forbes Bay 7114
Castle Hill (NSW) 2154
Castleburn 3862
Castlecrag 2068
Castlefield 3188
Castlemaine 3450
Castlereagh 2750
Castra Central 7315
Casuarina (NT) 5792
Casuarina (WA) 6167
Casuarina Sands (ACT) 2611
Casula 2170
Catagunya 7140
Catamaran 7116
Cathcart (NSW) 2632
Catherine Field 2171
Catherine Hill Bay 2301
Cathkin 3714
Cathundral 2823
Cattai 2756
Caulfield 3162
Caulfield East 3145
Caulfield North 3161
Caulfield South 3162
Caupaul 3312
Cavan 5094
Cavendish 3408
Caversham 6055
Caves Beach 2281
Caveside 7304
Cawongla 2474
Cecil Park 2171
Cecil Plains 4407
Cedar Creek (Beenleigh-QLD) 4207
Cedar Creek (Samford-QLD) 4520
Cedar Party Creek 2429
Ceduna 5690
Cement Mills 4352
Centenary Heights 4350
Centennial Park 2021
Central McDonald 2255
Central Park Via Caulfield East 3145
Central Park Via Glen Iris 3146
Central Tilba 2546
Centreville 3977
Cervantes 6511
Cessnock 2325
Cethana 7306
Chadoora 6213
Chadstone 3148
Chakola 2630
Chambers Flat 4133
Chandler 4155
Chandlers Creek 3889
Chapel Hill 4069
Chapman (ACT) 2611
Chapple Vale 3239
Charam 3318
Charbon 2848
Charlerol 3695
Charleston 5244
Charlestown 2290
Charleville 4470
Charleville Rail 4471
Charleyong 2622
Charlotte Pass 2630
Charlton 3525
Charmhaven 2263
Charnwood (ACT) 2615
Charters Towers 4820
Chartwell 3030
Chasm Creek 7320
Chatham (NSW) 2430
Chatswood 2067
Chatswood West 2066
Chatsworth (NSW) 2759
Chatsworth (VIC) 3291
Chatsworth Island 2460
Cheepie 4475
Cheero Point 2254
Cheesemans Creek 2800
Cheetara 6225
Chelmer 4068
Chelsea 3196
Cheltenham (NSW) 2119
Cheltenham (SA) 5014
Cheltenham (VIC) 3192
Chepstowe 3351
Cherbourg 4605
Chermside 4032
Cherry Gardens 5157
Cherrybrook 2120
Cherryville 5154
Cheshunt 3678
Chester Hill 2162
Chetwynd 3312
Chevron Island 4217
Chewton 3451
Chidlow 6556
Chifley (ACT) 2606
Chifley (NSW) 2036
Chigwell 7011
Childers (QLD) 4660
Childers (VIC) 3824
Chillagoe 4871
Chillingham 2484
Chillingollah 3585
Chiltern 3683
Chilwell 3220
Chinchilla 4413
Chinderah 2487
Chinkapook 3546
Chintin 3756
Chippendale 2008
Chipping Norton 2170
Chirn Park 4215
Chirnside Park 3116
Chisholm (ACT) 2905
Chisholm Centre 2153
Chiswick 2046
Chittaway Point 2259
Chittering 6084
Chorkerup 6330
Chowerup 6244
Christie Downs 5164
Christies 3962
Christies Beach 5165
Christmas Hills (TAS) 7330
Christmas Hills (VIC) 3775
Christmas Island (Indian Ocean) 6798
Chudleigh 7304
Chullora 2190
Chum Creek 3777
Church Point 2105
Churchill (QLD) 4305
Churchill (VIC) 3842
Churchlands 6018
City Beach 6015
City Rd P.O. (Sth Melb) 3205
Civic Square (ACT) Private Boxes Only 2608
Clackline 6564
Clagiraba 4211
Clandulla 2848
Clapham 5062
Clare (SA) 5453
Claredale 4807
Claremont (TAS) 7011
Claremont (WA) 6010
Clarence Gardens 5039
Clarence Park 5034
Clarence Point 7251
Clarence Street PO 2000
Clarence Town 2321
Clarendon 7212
Clarendon (NSW) 2756
Clarendon (SA) 5157
Clarendon (VIC) 3357
Clarendon Vale 7019
Clareville Beach 2107
Clarinda 3169
Clarkefield 3430
Clarkes Hill 3352
Clarkson 6030
Claude Road 7306
Clayfield 4011
Claymore 2560
Clayton 3168
Clayton (SA) 5256
Clayton South 3169
Clear Lake 3401
Clear Mountain 4500
Clearview 5085
Clematis 3782
Clemton Park 2206
Clergate 2800

Clermont 4721
Cleve 5640
Cleveland 7211
Cleveland (QLD) 4163
Clifton (NSW) 2515
Clifton (QLD) 4361
Clifton Beach (QLD) 4871
Clifton Beach (TAS) 7020
Clifton Gardens 2088
Clifton Hill (VIC) 3068
Clifton Springs 3222
Clifton Vale 7030
Cloncurry 4824
Clontarf (NSW) 2093
Clontarf (QLD) 4019
Closeburn 4520
Clovelly 2031
Clovelly Park 5042
Clover Flat 3315
Cloverdale (WA) 6105
Cloyna 4605
Cluan 7303
Club Terrace 3889
Clunes (NSW) 2480
Clunes (VIC) 3370
Clybucca 2440
Clyde (NSW) 2142
Clyde (VIC) 3978
Clydesdale (VIC) 3461
Coal Point 2283
Coalcliff 2508
Coalfalls 4305
Coalville 3825
Coatesville 3165
Cobar 2835
Cobargo 2547
Cobbadah 2347
Cobbannah 3862
Cobbitty 2570
Cobbora 2844
Cobden 3266
Cobdogla 5346
Cobram 3644
Cobungra 3898
Coburg 3058
Cockatoo 3781
Cockatoo Island 2000
Cockatoo Valley 5351
Cockburn (SA) 5440
Coconut Grove (NT) 5792
Cocos (Keeling) Islands
6799
Codrington 3285
Coen 4871
Coffin Bay 5607
Coffs Harbour 2450

Coffs Harbour Beach 2450
Coghills Creek 3364
Cohuna 3568
Coimadai 3337
Colac 3250
Colac Colac 3707
Colbinabbin 3559
Coldstream (VIC) 3770
Coleambally 2707
Colebrook 7027
Coledale 2515
Coleraine 3315
Coles Bay 7215
Colignan 3494
Colinton (QLD) 4306
Collarenebri 2833
Collaroy 2097
Collaroy Plateau 2098
Collector 2581
College Park 5069
Collerina 2839
Collie (NSW) 2827
Collie (WA) 6225
Collie Cardiff 6225
Collingullie 2652
Collingwood 3066
Collingwood Park 4301
Collins Cap 7012
Collinsvale (TAS) 7012
Collinsville (QLD) 4804
Collinswood 5081
Colliver 3630
Collombatti 2440
Colly Blue 2343
Colo 2756
Colo Vale 2575
Colonel Light Gardens
5041
Colyton 2760
Comara 2440
Combara 2829
Combienbar 3889
Comboyne 2429
Come-By-Chance 2832
Comet 4702
Comet Hill 3556
Comleroy Road 2758
Como (NSW) 2226
Como (WA) 6152
Conara 7211
Conargo 2710
Concord 2137
Concord North 2138
Concord Repatriation
Hospital 2139
Concord West 2138

Condah 3303
Condamine 4416
Condell Park 2200
Condobolin 2877
Condon 4815
Condong 2484
Congewai 2325
Congupna 3633
Coniston 2500
Conjola 2539
Connelleys Marsh 7173
Connells Point 2221
Connewarre 3227
Connewirricoo 3315
Conningham 7154
Connolly 6027
Conoble 2878
Conway 4800
Coober Pedy 5723
Coobowie 5583
Coochiemudlo 4163
Cooee 7320
Cooee Bay 4703
Cooerwull 2790
Coogee (NSW) 2034
Coogee Beach 6166
Cook (ACT) 2614
Cook (SA) 5710
Cookamidgera 2806
Cookardinia 2650
Cooke Plains 5261
Cooks Hill (Newcastle)
2300
Cooktown 4871
Coolabah 2831
Coolac (NSW) 2727
Cooladdi 4479
Coolah 2843
Coolamon 2701
Coolangatta (QLD) 4225
Coolaroo 3048
Coolatai 2402
Coolbellup 6163
Coolbinia 6050
Coolgardie 6429
Coolongolook 2423
Cooloongup 6168
Cooltong 5341
Coolum Beach 4573
Coolup 6214
Cooma (NSW) 2630
Cooma (VIC) 3616
Coomandook 5261
Coombabah 4216
Coombell 2470
Coomberdale 6512
Coomboona 3629
Coomera 4210
Coominya 4311
Coomoora 3461
Coonabarabran 2357
Coonalpyn 5265
Coonamble 2829
Coonans Hill 3044
Coonawarra 5263
Coonawarra Naval Base
(NT) 5789
Coonooer Bridge 3478
Coopernook 2426
Coopers Plains 4108
Coorabie 5690
Cooran 4569
Cooranbong 2265
Cooranga North 4408
Coorow 6515
Cooroy 4563
Coorparoo 4151
Cootamundra 2590
Cooyar 4402
Copacabana 2251
Cope Cope 3480
Copeland 2422
Copeton 2360

Copeville 5308
Copley 5732
Copmanhurst 2460
Copping 7174
Cora Lynn 3814
Corack 3480
Coradjil 3256
Coragulac 3249
Coraki 2471
Coramba 2450
Corangamite 3249
Corbie Hill 2705
Cordalba 4660
Cordeaux Heights 2526
Cordelia 4850
Corella 4570
Corfield 4733
Corinda 4075
Corindhap 3352
Corindi Beach 2456
Corinella 3984
Corinna 7321
Corio 3214
Corlette 2301
Corndale (NSW) 2480
Cornelian Bay 7008
Cornubia 4130
Cornwall 7215
Cornwallis 2756
Corny Point 5577
Corobimilla 2700
Coromandel Valley 5051
Coronet Bay 3984
Corop 3559
Cororooke 3254
Corowa 2646
Corra Linn 7250
Corrigin 6375
Corrimal 2518
Corroba 2295
Corrowidgin 2633
Corryong 3707
Corunnun 3249
Cosgrove 3645
Costerfield 3523
Cotham 3101
Cottage Point 2084
Cottesloe 6011
Cotton Tree 4558
Cottonvale 4375
Couangalt 3437
Coulta 5607
Couridjah 2571
Coutts Crossing 2460
Cowan (NSW) 2252
Cowan Cowan (QLD)
4025
Cowandilla 5033
Cowangie 3506
Cowaramup 6284
Cowell 5602
Cowes 3922
Cowley 4871
Cowper 2460
Cowra 2794
Cowwarr 3857
Crabbes Creek 2483
Craboon 2844
Crabtree 7106
Cracow 4719
Cradle Mountain 7306
Cradoc 7109
Cradock (SA) 5432
Crafers 5152
Craigie (NSW) 2632
Craigie (WA) 6025
Craigieburn 3064
Craigmore 5114
Cranbourne 3977
Cranbrook 7190
Cranbrook (QLD) 4814
Cranbrook (WA) 6321
Cranebrook 2750

Cranley 4350
Craven 2422
Crawley 6009
Creek Junction 3669
Creighton 3666
Cremorne (NSW) 2090
Cremorne (TAS) 7024
Crescent Head 2440
Cressy (TAS) 7302
Cressy (VIC) 3322
Creswick 3363
Crib Point 3919
Crimea 3161
Cringila 2501
Croker Island 5791
Cromer (NSW) 2099
Cromer (VIC) 3193
Cronin Island 4217
Cronulla 2230
Crooble 2400
Crooked Corner 2583
Crooked River 3862
Crookwell 2583
Croppa Creek 2411
Cross Keys 3041
Cross Roads (NSW) 2170
Crossmaglen 2441
Crossover 3821
Crotty 7466
Croudace Bay 2280
Crowdy Head 2427
Crowlands 3377
Crows Nest (NSW) 2065
Crows Nest (QLD) 4355
Crowther 2803
Croxton 3070
Croxton East 3301
Croydon (NSW) 2132
Croydon (QLD) 4871
Croydon (SA) 5008
Croydon (VIC) 3136
Croydon Park (NSW)
2133
Cryon 2832
Crystal Brook (SA) 5523
Crystal Creek (NSW) 2484
Cuckoo 7254
Cudal 2864
Cudgee 3265
Cudgen 2487
Cudgera Creek 2484
Cudgewa 3705
Cudlee Creek 5232
Cudmirrah 2540
Cue (WA) 6640
Culburra 5261
Culburra Beach 2540
Culcairn 2660
Culgoa 3530
Cullacabardee 6067
Cullen Bullen 2790
Cullenswood 7215
Culloden 3860
Cullulleraine 3496
Cumberland Park (SA)
5041
Cumberland Park (VIC)
3844
Cumborah 2832
Cummins 5631
Cumnock 2867
Cundare 3251
Cunderdin 6407
Cundinup 6275
Cundle Flat 2424
Cundletown 2430
Cungena 5660
Cunjurong Point 2539
Cunnamulla 4490
Cuprona 7316
Curban 2827
Curdie Vale 3268
Curdies River 3268

Curl Curl 2096
Curl Curl North 2099
Curlewis (NSW) 2381
Curlewis (VIC) 3222
Curlwaa 2648
Currabubula 2342
Currajong (QLD) 4812
Currambine 6028
Curramulka 5580
Currarong 2540
Currency Creek 5214
Currie 7256
Currumbin 4223
Curtin (ACT) 2605
Curyo 3483
Cuthbert 6330
Cuttabri 2388
Cygnet 7112

D

Daceyville 2032
Dadswells Bridge 3385
Daglish 6008
Daguilar 4514
Daintree 4873
Dairy Plains 7304
Daisy Hill 4127
Dajarra 4825
Dakabin 4503
Dalby 4405
Dalby Forward 4406
Daleys Point 2256
Dalgety 2630
Dalkeith 6009
Dallas (VIC) 3047
Dalmeny 2546
Dalmore 3981
Dalrymple Heights 4757
Dalton 2581
Dalveen 4374
Dalwallinu 6609
Daly River 5791
Daly Waters 5780
Dalyston 3992
Dampier 6713
Dandaragan 6507
Dandenong 3175
Dandongadale 3737
Dangar 2309
Dangar Island 2253
Dangarfield 2336
Dangin 6383
Danyo 3512
Dapto 2530
Darbys Falls 2793
Dardadine 6392
Dardanup 6236
Darebin 3079
Dareton 2717
Dargalong 3608
Dargo 3862
Dark Corner 2795
Darkan 6392
Darke Peak 5642
Darkes Forest 2508
Darlimurla 3871
Darling Harbour 2009
Darling Heights 4350
Darling Point 2027
Darling Via Caulfield East
3145
Darling Via Glen Iris 3146
Darlinghurst 2010
Darlington (NSW) 2008
Darlington (SA) 5047
Darlington (VIC) 3271
Darlington (WA) 6070
Darlington Point 2706
Darnick 2878
Darnum 3822

Daroobalgie 2870
Darra 4076
Darradup 6275
Darraweit Guim 3756
Darriman 3851
Dartbrook 2336
Dartmoor 3304
Dartmouth (VIC) 3701
DARWIN
CITY 5790
GPO PRIVATE BOXES 5794
Darwin (Community And Private Bags) 5791
Davidson 2085
Davis (Antarctica) 7150
Davis Creek (Aberdeen) 2336
Davistown 2250
Daw Park 5041
Dawesville 6210
Dawsons Hill 2330
Dayboro 4521
Daylesford 3460
Daymar 4495
Daysdale 2646
Deagon 4017
Deakin (ACT) 2600
Deakin University (VIC) 3217
Dean 3352
Deanmill 6258
Deans Marsh 3235
Deception Bay 4508
Deddick 3888
Deddington 7212
Dederang 3691
Dee Lagoon 7140
Dee Why 2099
Deep Bay 7112
Deepdene Via Balwyn 3103
Deepdene Via Kew 3101
Deepwater 2371
Deer Park 3023
Deer Park East 3022
Deeragun 4816
Deeral 4871
Defence Forces 2890
Delamere 5204
Delegate 2633
Delegate River East 3888
Dellicknora 3888
Delmont 7301
Deloraine 7304
Delungra 2403
Denbarker 6324
Dendy 3186
Denham 6537
Deniliquin 2710
Denistone 2114
Denistone East 2112
Denman 2328
Denmark 6333
Dennes Point 7157
Dennington 3280
Dennis 3070
Derby (TAS) 7254
Derby (VIC) 3516
Derby (WA) 6728
Dereel 3352
Dergholm 3312
Dernancourt 5075
Derrimut Via Footscray West 3012
Derrimut Via Werribee 3030
Derrinallum 3325
Derriwong 2877
Derwent Bridge 7140
Derwent Park 7009
Detention River 7321
Detpa 3423
Devenish 3726
Devils Gate 7306
Deviot 7251
Devon Hills 7250
Devon North 3971
Devon Park 5008
Devonport 7310
Dharruk 2770
Dhurringile 3610
Diamond Creek 3089
Diamond Head 2443
Dianas Basin 7215
Dianella 6062
Diapur 3418
Dickson (ACT) 2602
Diddleum Plains 7257
Digby 3309
Diggers Rest 3427
Diggora West 3561
Dilston 7252
Dimboola 3414
Dimbulah 4872
Dingee 3571
Dingley 3172
Dingo 4702
Dingwall 3579
Dinmore 4303
Dinninup 6244
Dinoga 2404
Direk 5110
Dirranbandi 4486
Dixons Creek 3775
Dobroyd Head 2093
Dobroyd Point (Haberfield) 2045
Docker 3678
Dodges Ferry 7173
Dolans Bay 2229
Dollar 3871
Dolls Point 2219
Don 7310
Donald 3480
Doncaster 3108
Doncaster East 3109
Doncaster Heights 3109
Dongara 6525
Donnelly River Mill 6258
Donnybrook 3064
Donnybrook (NSW) 2790
Donnybrook (QLD) 4510
Donnybrook (WA) 6239
Donvale 3111
Doodlakine 6411
Dooen 3401
Dookie 3646
Dookie College 3647
Doolandella 4077
Doomadgee (QLD) 4830
Doomben 4007
Doon Doon 2484
Doonside 2767
Dooralong 2259
Dora Creek 2264
Doreen 3754
Dorodong 3312
Dorrigo 2453
Dorrington 4060
Dorroughby 2480
Double Bay 2028
Double Creek 7190
Doubleview 6018
Doubtful Creek 2470
Douglas 3401
Douglas Park 2569
Douglas River 7215
Dover 7116
Dover Gardens 5048
Dover Heights 2030
Doveton 3177
Dowerin 6461
Downer (ACT) 2602
Doyalson 2262
Drake 2470
Draper 4520
Drayton 4350
Dreeite 3249
Drewvale 4116
Drik Drik 3304
Drillham 4424
Dripstone 2820
Driver 5787
Dromana 3936
Dromedary 7030
Drouin 3818
Drumborg 3304
Drummond 3461
Drummoyne 2047
Dry Creek (SA) 5094
Drysdale 3222
Duaringa 4702
Dubbo 2830
Dublin 5501
Duchess 4825
Duckmaloi 2787
Dudinin 6363
Dudley 2290
Dudley Park 5008
Dudley South 3995
Duffy (ACT) 2611
Duffys Forest 2084
Dukin 6475
Dulacca 4425
Dulcot 7025
Dululu 4702
Dulverton 7305
Dulwich 5065
Dulwich Hill 2203
Dumbalk 3956
Dumbalk East 3957
Dumbleyung 6350
Dumosa 3527
Dunalley 7177
Dunbible Creek 2484
Dunbogan 2443
Dunbulbalane 3636
Duncraig 6023
Dundas 2117
Dundee 2370
Dundurnell 3271
Dundurrabin 2453
Dunearn 3175
Dunedoo 2844
Dungay 2484
Dungog 2420
Dungowan 2340
Dunheved 2760
Dunk Island 4816
Dunkeld (NSW) 2795
Dunkeld (VIC) 3294
Dunkirk 3630
Dunmore (NSW) 2529
Dunnstown 3352
Dunolly (VIC) 3472
Dunoon 2480
Dunorlan 7304
Dunrobin 3312
Dunsborough 6281
Duntroon (ACT) 2600
Dunwich 4163
Durack 4077
Dural 2158
Duramana 2795
Duranbah 2487
Duranillin 6393
Durham Lead 3352
Durham Ox 3576
Duri 2344
Durong South 4610
Durras 2536
Dutton Park 4102
Duverney 3323
Dwarda 6308
Dwellingup 6213
Dyers Crossing 2429
Dynnyrne 7005
Dyraaba Central 2470
Dysart 7030
Dysart (QLD) 4745

E

Eagle Farm 4007
Eagle Heights 4271
Eagle Junction 4011
Eagle On The Hill 5150
Eagle Point 3878
Eagle Vale 2558
Eagleby 4207
Eaglehawk 3556
Eaglehawk Neck 7179
Eaglemont Via Ivanhoe 3079
Eaglemont Via Rosanna 3084
Earlville 4870
Earlwood 2206
East Brisbane 4169
East Fremantle 6158
East Gresford 2311
East Hills 2213
East Keilor 3033
East Lynne 2536
East Maitland 2323
East Malvern Via Caulfield East 3145
East Malvern Via Glen Iris 3146
East Melbourne 3002
East Point (NT) 5790
East Risdon 7017
East Sale RAAF 3852
Eastbrook 6260
Eastern Creek (NSW) 2766
Eastern Heights 4305
Eastern View 3221
Eastlakes (Rosebery) 2018
Eastville (VIC) 3463
Eastwood (NSW) 2122
Eastwood (SA) 5063
Eastwood (TAS) 7018
Eaton 6230
Eatons Hill 4037
Ebbw Vale 4304
Ebden 3691
Ebenezer 2756
Ebor 2453
Echuca 3564
Echunga 5153
Ecklin South 3265
Eddington 3472
Eddystone Point 7254
Eden 2551
Eden Hill (WA) 6054
Eden Hills (SA) 5050
Eden Park (VIC) 3757
Eden Valley 5235
Edenhope 3318
Edensor Park 2176
Edge Hill 4870
Edgecliff 2027
Edgecombe 3444
Edgeroi 2391
Edgewater 6027
Edgeworth 2285
Edi 3678
Edillilie 5630
Edinburgh RAAF (SA) 5111
Edith 2787
Edith Creek 7330
Edithburgh 5583
Edithvale 3196
Edmonton 4869
Edward River 4871
Edwardstown (SA) 5039
Eganstown 3461
Egg And Bacon Bay 7112
Egg Lagoon 7256
Eglinton (NSW) 2795
Eglinton (WA) 6034
Eidsvold 4627
Eight Mile Plains 4123
Eildon (VIC) 3713
Einasleigh 4871
Ejanding 6464
Ekibin 4121
El Arish 4855
Elaine 3334
Elands 2429
Elanora 4221
Elanora Heights 2101
Elderslie 7030
Elderslie (Branxton) 2335
Elderslie (Camden) 2570
Eldon 7027
Eldorado 3746
Electrona 7100
Eleebana 2280
Elgin 6237
Elimbah 4516
Elizabeth 5112
Elizabeth Bay (Potts Point) 2011
Elizabeth Downs 5113
Elizabeth Field 5113
Elizabeth North 5113
Elizabeth Park 5113
Elizabeth Town 7304
Elizabeth West 5113
Ellalong 2325
Ellam 3423
Ellaswood 3875
Elleker 6330
Ellenborough 2446
Ellendale 7140
Ellengrove 4077
Ellerslie (VIC) 3265
Ellerston 2337
Elliminyt 3249
Elliott (NT) 5760
Elliott (TAS) 7325
Elliott Heads 4670
Elliston 5670
Elmhurst 3469
Elmore 3558
Elong Elong 2831
Elphin 7250
Elphinstone 3448
Elsmore 2370
Elsternwick 3185
Eltham (NSW) 2480
Eltham (VIC) 3095
Elvina Bay 2105
Elwick 7010
Elwood 3184
Embleton 6062
Emerald (QLD) 4720
Emerald (VIC) 3782
Emerton 2770
Emita 7255
Emmaville 2371
Empire Bay 2256
Empire Vale 2478
Emu 3475
Emu Creek 3551
Emu Flat 3522
Emu Heights 7320
Emu Park 4702
Emu Plains 2750
Emu Point 6330
Emu Vale 4371
Endeavour Hills 3802
Endsleigh 2800
Eneabba 6518
Enfield (NSW) 2136
Enfield South 2133
Enfield (SA) 5085
Enfield (VIC) 3352
Engadine 2233
Englefield 3407
English Town 7212
Enmore 2042
Enngonia 2840
Enoggera 4051
Enoggera Mil. P.O. 4052
Ensay 3895
Eppalock 3551
Epping (NSW) 2121
Epping (VIC) 3076
Epping Forest (TAS) 7257
Epsom 3551
Eraring 2264
Ercildoune 3352
Erica 3825
Erigolia 2669
Erikin 6386
Erina 2250
Erina Heights 2260
Erindale 5066
Erinunderra 3889
Ermington 2115
Ernabella (NT) 5751
Ernest 4214
Eromanga 4480
Erowal Bay 2540
Erriba 7310
Erskine Park 2759
Erskineville 2043
Eschol Park 2558
Esk 4312
Eskdale (VIC) 3701
Esperance 6450
Essendon 3040
Essendon Airport 3041
Ethelton 5015
Eton 4741
Ettalong Beach 2257
Ettrick 2474
Euabalong 2877
Eubenangee 4860
Euchareena 2866
Eucumbene 2630
Eudlo 4554
Eudunda 5374
Eugenana 7310
Eugowra 2806
Eulo 4491
Eumundi 4562
Eumungerie 2831
Eungai Creek 2441
Eungai Rail 2441
Eungella 2484
Euramo 4854
Euratha 2669
Eureka (NSW) 2480
Eureka (VIC) 3350
Euroa 3666
Eurobin 3739
Eurobin Falls 3740
Euston 2739
Evandale (SA) 5069
Evandale (TAS) 7212
Evans Head 2473
Evansford 3371
Evanston (SA) 5116
Evatt (ACT) 2617
Evelyn Central 4872
Everard Park 5035
Everton 3746
Everton Hills 4053
Everton Park 4053
Ewey Bay 2228
Exeter (NSW) 2679
Exeter (SA) 5019
Exeter (TAS) 7251

Exford 3338
Exmouth 6707
Exton 7303

F

Fadden (ACT) 2904
Failford 2430
Fairbridge 6208
Fairfield (NSW) 2165
Fairfield (QLD) 4103
Fairfield (VIC) 3078
Fairhaven 3221
Fairhope 3875
Fairlight 2094
Fairvale 2165
Fairview Park 5126
Fairy Dell 3561
Fairy Hill (NSW) 2470
Fairy Meadow 2519
Falcon 6210
Falls Creek (NSW) 2540
Falls Creek (VIC) 3699
Falmouth 7215
Fannie Bay (NT) 5790
Faraday Park 2114
Farleigh 4741
Farley 2320
Farmborough Heights 2526
Farnham 2820
Farrell Flat 5416
Farrer (ACT) 2607
Fassifern 2283
Faulconbridge 2776
Faversham 3127
Fawkner 3060
Federal 2480
Felixstow 5070
Fennell Bay 2283
Fentonbury 7140
Fentons Creek 3518
Ferguson (WA) 6236
Fern Bay 2295
Fern Hill (VIC) 3458
Fern Tree 7101
Fernbank 3864
Ferndale (WA) 6155
Fernihurst 3536
Fernleigh 2479
Fernmount 2454
Ferntree Gully 3156
Fernvale 4306
Ferny Creek 3786
Ferny Grove 4055
Ferny Hills 4055
Ferryden Park 5010
Fiddle Town 2159
Fifield 2875
Fig Tree Pocket 4069
Figtree 2525
Fimiston 6433
Finch Hatton 4756
Findon 5023
Fine Flower Creek 2460
Fingal (NSW) 2487
Fingal (TAS) 7214
Fingal Head 2487
Finke 5751
Finley 2713
Finniss 5255
Firefly 2429
Firle 507C
Fish Creek 3959
Fisher (ACT) 2611
Fishermans Bend 3207
Fishing Point 2283
Fitzgerald 7140
Fitzgibbon 4034
Fitzroy (SA) 5082
Fitzroy (VIC) 3065
Fitzroy Crossing 6765
Fitzroy Falls 2577
Five Dock 2046
Five Ways 3977
Flaggy Creek 3875
Flaggy Rock 4741
Flagstaff Gully 7015
Flagstaff Hill 5159
Flaxley (SA) 5153
Flemington (NSW) 2140
Flemington (VIC) 3031
Flemington Markets 2129
Flinders (VIC) 3929
Flinders Bay 6290
Flinders Island 7255
Flinders Naval Depot 3920
Flinders Park (SA) 5025
Flinders Park (WA) 6330
Flinders View 4305
Floraville 2280
Floreat 6014
Floreat Forum 6014
Florey (ACT) 2615
Flowerdale (TAS) 7325
Flowerdale (VIC) 3717
Flowerpot 7100
Flowery Gully 7251
Flying Fish Point 4860
Flynn (ACT) 2615
Flynn (VIC) 3844
Flynns Beach 2444
Footscray 3011
Forbes (NSW) 2871
Forcett 7173
Fords Bridge 2840
Forest 7330
Forest Grove 6286
Forest Hill (QLD) 4342
Forest Hill (VIC) 3131
Forest Hill (WA) 6324
Forest Lodge 2037
Forest Range 5139
Forest Reefs 2798
Forester 7254
Forestville (NSW) 2087
Forestville (SA) 5035
Forge Creek 3875
Forrest (ACT) 2603
Forrest (VIC) 3236
Forrest (WA) 6434
Forrestdale 6112
Forresters Beach 2260
Forrestfield 6058
Forsayth 4871
Forster (NSW) 2428
Fortescue Bay 7182
Forth 7310
Fortitude Valley 4006
Foster (VIC) 3960
Fosterville 3557
Fountain Gate 3805
Four Mile Creek 2800
Foxground 2534
Framlingham 3265
Frances 5262
Frankford 7251
Frankland 6396
Franklin 7113
Franklin Village 7249
Franklinford 3461
Frankston 3199
Frankston North 3200
Fraser (ACT) 2615
Fraser (VIC) 3630
Frederickton 2440
Freeburgh 3741
Freeling 5372
Freemans Reach 2756
Freemans Waterhole 2323
Fregon 5751
Fremantle (WA) 6160
French Park 2655
Frenchman Bay 6330
Frenchs Forest 2086
Frenchs Road 2068
Frenchville 4701
Freshwater (QLD) 4872
Freshwater Creek (VIC) 3216
Frewville 5063
Frodsley 7214
Fruitgrove 4113
Fryerstown 3451
Fulham (SA) 5024
Fulham (VIC) 3851
Fullarton (SA) 5063
Fullers Bridge 2067
Fullerton (NSW) 2583
Fullerton Cove 2301
Fumina 3825
Furracabad 2370
Fyansford 3221
Fyshwick (ACT) 2609

G

GPO Private Boxes Perth (WA) 6001
Gabbin 6476
Gabo Island 3889
Gaffneys Creek 3723
Gagebrook 7030
Gailes 4300
Gairdner 6337
Galah 3506
Galaquil 3395
Galga 5308
Galiwinku 5791
Galloways Hill 4171
Galong 2585
Galore 2652
Galston 2159
Ganmain 2702
Gannons Creek 2446
Gapsted 3737
Garah 2405
Garbutt 4814
Garden City (VIC) 3207
Garden Island (NSW) 2000
Garden Island (WA) 6168
Garden Island Creek 7112
Garden Suburb 2289
Gardenvale Via Brighton East 3187
Gardenvale Via Elsternwick 3185
Gardiner 3146
Gardners Bay 7112
Garema 2871
Garfield (VIC) 3814
Gargett 4741
Garland 2797
Garra 2866
Garradunga 4860
Garran (ACT) 2605
Garthowen 2345
Garvoc 3265
Gascoyne Junction 6705
Gateshead 2290
Gatton 4343
Gatum 3407
Gaven 4211
Gawler (SA) 5118
Gawler (TAS) 7315
Gayndan 4625
Gaythorne 4051
Geebung 4034
Geelong 3220
Geelong East 3219
Geelong North 3215
Geelong West 3218
Geeveston 7116
Geilston Bay 7015
Gelantipy 3885
Gellibrand River 3239
Gelliondale 3971
Gelorup 6230
Gemalla 2795
Gembrook 3783
Geneva 2474
Genoa 3889
George Town (TAS) 7253
Georges Hall 2198
Georges Heights 2088
Georges Plains 2795
Georgetown (NSW) 2298
Georgetown (QLD) 4871
Georgetown (SA) 5472
Georgica 2480
Gepps Cross 5094
Geraldton 6530
Gerang Gerung 3417
Gerangamete 3243
Geranium 5301
Gerogery 2642
Gerringong 2534
Gerroa 2534
Geurie 2831
Gheringhap 3331
Ghinni Ghinni 2430
Ghooli 6426
Gibson 6448
Gidgegannup 6555
Gilberton (QLD) 4208
Gilberton (SA) 5081
Gilderoy 3797
Gilead 2560
Gilfillan 6225
Gilgai 2360
Gilgandra 2827
Gillenbah 2700
Gilles Plains 5086
Gillieston 3616
Gillieston Heights 2321
Gillingarra 6510
Gillman 5013
Gilmore (ACT) 2905
Gilmore (NSW) 2720
Gilston 4211
Gin Gin (QLD) 4671
Gingin (WA) 6503
Gingkin 2787
Ginninderra (ACT) 2617
Gipsy Point 3889
Giralang (ACT) 2617
Girgarre 3624
Girilambone 2831
Girral 2669
Girraween (NSW) 2145
Girrawheen (WA) 6064
Giru 4809
Girvan 2425
Gisborne 3437
Gladesville 2111
Gladstone (NSW) 2440
Gladstone (QLD) 4680
Gladstone (SA) 5473
Gladstone (TAS) 7254
Gladstone Park 3043
Gladysdale 3797
Glance Creek 7321
Glandore 5037
Glanville 5015
Glasshouse Mountains 4518
Glaziers Bay 7112
Glebe (NSW) 2037
Glebe (TAS) 7000
Glen Alice 2849
Glen Alpine 2560
Glen Alvie 3979
Glen Aplin 4381
Glen Creek 3691
Glen Davis 2846
Glen Fern 7140
Glen Forbes 3990
Glen Forrest 6071
Glen Huon 7109
Glen Innes 2370
Glen Iris (VIC) 3146
Glen Osmond (SA) 5064
Glen Valley (VIC) 3898
Glen Waverley 3150
Glen William 2321
Glenaladale 3864
Glenalta 5052
Glenarbon 4385
Glenaroua 3764
Glenbervie 3040
Glenbrook 2773
Glenburn 3717
Glencoe (NSW) 2365
Glencoe (SA) 5291
Glendale 2285
Glendalough 6016
Glenden 4743
Glendevie 7116
Glendhu 7249
Glendonbrook 2330
Glenelg 5045
Glenella 4741
Glenfallock 3858
Glenferrie 3122
Glenfield (NSW) 2167
Glenfield (WA) 6532
Glenfyne 3266
Glengarry (TAS) 7251
Glengarry (VIC) 3854
Glengowrie 5044
Glenhaven 2154
Glenhuntly Via Carnegie 3163
Glenhuntly Via Caulfield South 3162
Glenisla 3408
Glenloth 3527
Glenluce 3451
Glenlusk 7012
Glenlyon 3461
Glenmaggie 3858
Glenmore (VIC) 3340
Glenmorgan 4423
Glennie Heights 4370
Glennies Creek 2330
Glenora 7140
Glenorchy (TAS) 7010
Glenorchy (VIC) 3385
Glenore Grove 4342
Glenorie 2157
Glenormiston 3265
Glenreagh 2450
Glenrowan 3675
Glenroy (VIC) 3046
Glenside 5065
Glenthompson 3293
Glenunga 5064
Glenvale (QLD) 4350
Glenvale (VIC) 3757
Glossodia 2756
Glossop 5344
Gloucester 2422
Glynde 5070
Gnarkeet 3324
Gnarpurt 3324
Gnarwarre (VIC) 3221
Gnotuk 3260
Gnowangerup 6335
Gnowellen 6328
Gobarralong 2727
Gobur 3719
Gogango 4702
Gol Gol 2739
Golconda 7254
Golden Beach (QLD) 4551
Golden Grove 5125
Golden Hill 6333
Golden Square 3555
Golden Valley 7304
Goldsworthy 6723
Golspie 2580

Thomas Cambridge Sen., colonial era letter carrier at Windsor, NSW.

Gongolgon 2839
Goode Beach 6330
Goodna 4300
Goodnight 2739
Goodooga 2838
Goodwood (SA) 5034
Goodwood (TAS) 7010
Goolgowi 2652
Goolma 2852
Goolmangar 2480
Gooloogong 2805
Goolwa 5214
Goomalling 6460
Goombungee 4354
Goomburra 4362
Goomeri 4601
Goon Nure 3875
Goondi 4860
Goondiwindi 4390
Goonellabah 2480
Goonengerry 2482
Goongarrie 6431
Goongerah 3888
Goonumbla 2870
Gooram 3666
Gooramadda 3685
Goorambat 3725
Goornong 3557
Gooseberry Hill 6076
Goovigen 4702
Gorae 3306
Gordon (NSW) 2072
Gordon (TAS) 7164
Gordon (VIC) 3345
Gordon Park 4031
Gordonvale 4865
Gore 4352
Gore Hill 2065
Gormandale 3873
Gormanston 7466
Gorokan 2263
Goroke 3412
Gosford 2250
Goshen 7216
Gosnells 6110
Goughs Bay 3723
Goulbourn Island 5791
Goulburn 2580
Goulburn Weir 3608
Goulds Country 7216
Gowangardie 3669
Gowrie 2904
Gowrie (Singleton - NSW) 2330
Gowrie (Tamworth - NSW) 2340
Gowrie Park 7306
Grabben Gullen 2583
Gracemere 4702
Graceville 4075
Grafton 2460
Graham 3207
Grahamstown (Adelong) 2729
Grahamvale 3630
Graman 2360
Grandchester 4340
Grange (QLD) 4051
Grange (SA) 5022
Grangeburn 3300
Grantham 4347
Granton 7030
Grantville (VIC) 3984
Granville (NSW) 2142
Granville (QLD) 4650
Granya 3701
Grass Patch 6446
Grass Valley 6403
Grassdale 3302
Grassmere 3282
Grasstree Hill 7017
Grassy 7256
Gravelly Beach 7251
Gravesend 2401
Grawin 2832
Gray (TAS) 7215
Gray (NT) 5787
Graylands 6010
Grays Point 2232
Graytown 3608
Gre Gre 3478
Great Bay 7156
Great Marlow 2460
Great Western 3377
Gredgwin 3537
Green Fields 5107
Green Gully 3462
Green Hill (NSW) 2440
Green Island 4871
Green Point (Gosford) 2250
Greenacre (NSW) 2190
Greenacres (SA) 5086
Greenbank 4124
Greenbushes 6254
Greendale (NSW) 2750
Greendale (VIC) 3341
Greenethorpe 2809
Greenfield Park 2176
Greenhill 5140
Greenland 2330
Greenmount (Coolangatta-QLD) 4225
Greenmount (QLD) 4359
Greenmount (WA) 6056
Greenock 5360
Greenough 6530
Greens Beach 7251
Greens Creek 3381
Greensborough 3088
Greenslopes 4120
Greenvale (QLD) 4816
Greenvale (VIC) 3047
Greenwald 3304
Greenways 5272
Greenwell Point 2540
Greenwich 2065
Greenwith 5125
Greenwood 6024
Gregson 7017
Grenfell 2810
Gresford 2311
Greta (NSW) 2334
Greta (VIC) 3675
Gretna 7140
Grevillia 2474
Greystanes 2145
Greythorn 3104
Griffin 4503
Griffith (ACT) 2603
Griffith (NSW) 2680
Griffith University (QLD) 4111
Grimwade 6253
Grindelwald 7251
Gringegalgona 3315
Grogan 2666
Grong Grong 2652
Grose Vale 2753
Grose Wold 2753
Grosvenor Street PO 2000
Grove 7106
Grovedale 3216
Grovely 4054
Guanaba 4210
Gubbata 2669
Guilderton 6041
Guildford (NSW) 2161
Guildford (VIC) 3451
Guildford (WA) 6055
Guildford Junction 7321
Guildford North 2160
Gulargambone 2828
Gulgong 2852
Gulliver 4812
Gulnare 5471
Gulpa 2710
Guluguba 4418
Gum Flat 2360
Gum Scrub 2441
Gumdale 4154
Gumeracha 5233
Gumly Gumly 2652
Gunalda 4570
Gunbar 2711
Gunbower 3566
Gundagai 2722
Gundaroo 2620
Gundillion 2622
Gundowring 3691
Gundy 2337
Gungal 2333
Gunn (NT) 5786
Gunnamatta Bay 2230
Gunnedah 2380
Gunning 2581
Gunningbland 2876
Gunns Plains 7315
Gunpowder 4825
Gununa 4871
Gurley 2398
Gutha 6623
Guthalungra 4805
Guthridge 3850
Guyra 2365
Guys Forest 3709
Guys Hill 3807
Gwabegar 2356
Gwambygine 6302
Gwandalan 2259
Gwelup 6018
Gwynneville 2500
Gymbowen 3401
Gymea 2227
Gympie 4570

H

HMAS Cerberus Western Port 3920
Haberfield 2045
Hackett (ACT) 2602
Hacketts 6014
Hacketts Gully 6076
Hackham 5163
Hackney 5069
Haddon (VIC) 3351
Haden (QLD) 4352
Hadfield 3046
Hadspen 7257
Hagley 7257
Hahndorf 5245
Halekulani 2262
Halfway Creek 2460
Halidon 5309
Halifax 4850
Hall (ACT) 2618
Hallett 5419
Hallett Cove 5158
Hallidays Point 2430
Halls Creek (WA) 6770
Halls Gap 3381
Hallston 3953
Halton 2311
Hamelin Pool 6532
Hamersley 6022
Hamilton (TAS) 7140
Hamilton (NSW) 2303
Hamilton (QLD) 4007
Hamilton (SA) 5373
Hamilton (VIC) 3300
Hamilton Hill 6163
Hamilton Island 4803
Hamley Bridge 5401
Hamlyn Heights 3215
Hammond (SA) 5430
Hammondville 2170
Hammondville East 2171
Hampshire 7321
Hampstead Gardens 5086
Hampton (NSW) 2790
Hampton (VIC) 3188
Hampton Park (VIC) 3976
Hannaford 4406
Hannam Vale 2443
Hansonville 3675
Hanwood 2680
Happy Valley (QLD) 4825
Happy Valley (SA) 5159
Harbord 2096
Harcourt 3453
Harden 2587
Hardys Bay 2256
Hardys Mill 2653
Harefield 2650
Harewood 6333
Harford 7307
Hargraves 2850
Harkaway 3806
Harlaxton 4350
Harlin 4306
Harman (ACT) 2600
Harrietville 3741
Harrington 2427
Harris Park 2150
Harrismith 6361
Harristown 4350
Harrisville 4307
Harrow 3317
Harston 3616
Hartley (NSW) 2790
Hartwell Via Burwood 3125
Hartwell Via Camberwell 3124
Harvey 6220
Harwood Island 2465
Haslam 5680
Hassall 2770
Hastings (TAS) 7116
Hastings (VIC) 3915
Hastings Point 2489
Hat Head 2440
Hatfield 2715
Hatherleigh 5280
Hattah 3501
Haven 3401
Havenview 7320
Havilah (NSW) 2850
Hawker (ACT) 2614
Hawker (SA) 5434
Hawkesbury Agricultural College 2753
Hawkesdale 3287
Hawkhurst 3862
Hawkinston 3578
Hawks Nest 2324
Hawksburn Via South Yarra 3141
Hawksburn Via Toorak 3142
Hawley Beach 7307
Hawthorn (SA) 5062
Hawthorn (VIC) 3122
Hawthorn East 3123
Hawthorn South Via Camberwell 3124
Hawthorn South Via Hawthorn East 3123
Hawthorndene 5051
Hawthorne (QLD) 4171
Hay 2711
Hayes 7140
Hayman Island 4741
Haymarket 2000
Hazelbrook 2779
Hazeldene 3658
Hazelgrove 2787
Hazelmere 6055
Hazelvale 6333
Hazelwood Park (SA) 5066
Healesville 3777
Healy 4825
Hearson 6715
Heathcote (VIC) 3523
Heathcote (NSW) 2233
Heathcote Junction 3758
Heatherbrae 2324
Heatherdale Via Mitcham 3132
Heatherdale Via Ringwood 3134
Heatherton 3202
Heatherton Via Cheltenham 3192
Heathfield 5153
Heathmere 3305
Heathmont 3135
Heathpool 5068
Heathridge 6027
Heathwood (QLD) 4110
Heathwood (VIC) 3134
Heatley 4814
Hebden 2330
Hebel 4486
Hebersham 2770
Heckenberg 2168
Hectorville 5073
Heddon Greta 2321
Hedley 3967
Heidelberg 3084
Heidelberg Heights 3081
Heidelberg Repatriation General Hospital 3081
Heka 7315
Helena Valley 6056
Helensburgh 2508
Helensvale 4210
Helidon 4344
Hemmant 4174
Henderson 6166
Hendon (SA) 5014
Hendra 4011
Henley 2111
Henley Beach 5022
Henley Brook 6055
Henrietta 7321
Henty (NSW) 2658
Henty (VIC) 3312
Hepburn Springs 3461
Herberton 4872
Hermannsburg 5751
Hermidale 2831
Hermit Park 4812
Hernani 2453
Herne Hill (VIC) 3218
Herne Hill (WA) 6056
Hernes Oak 3838
Heron Island 4680
Herons Creek 2443
Herrick 7254
Herston 4006
Hesket 3442
Hesse 3221
Hester 6255
Hetherington 4680
Hewitt 2759
Hexham (NSW) 2322
Hexham (VIC) 3273
Heybridge 7316
Heyfield 3858
Heywood 3304
Hibbard 2444
Hickeys Creek 2440
Hicksborough 3995
Hidden Valley (QLD) 4816
Higgins (ACT) 2615
High Camp Plain 3764
High Wycombe 6057
Highbury (SA) 5089
Highbury (WA) 6313
Highclere 7321
Highcroft 7183
Highett 3190
Highfields (NSW) 2289
Highfields (QLD) 4352
Highgate (SA) 5063
Highgate (WA) 6000
Highgate Hill 4101
Highpoint West 3032
Highton 3216
Highvale 4520
Hill End (NSW) 2850
Hill End (QLD) 4101
Hill End (VIC) 3825
Hillarys 6025
Hillas Creek 2729
Hillbank 5112
Hillcrest (TAS) 7320
Hillcrest (SA) 5086
Hillcrest (VIC) 3351
Hilldale Via Dungog 2420
Hillgrove 2350
Hillier (SA) 5116
Hillman 6168
Hillsdale Via Matraville 2036
Hillside (VIC) 3875
Hillston 2675
Hilltop (Mittagong) 2575
Hilltown 5455
Hillwood 7252
Hilton (SA) 5033
Hilton (WA) 6163
Hindmarsh 5007
Hines Hill 6413
Hinnomunjie 3898
Hinton 2321
Hivesville 4612
HOBART
CITY 7000
GPO PRIVATE BOXES 7001
Hobartville 2753
Hobbys Yards 2795
Hoddles Creek 3139
Holbrook 2644
Holden Hill 5088
Holder (ACT) 2611
Holland Park 4121
Hollisdale 2446
Hollow Tree 7140
Holloway Beach 4871
Hollydeen 2333
Hollywell 4216
Hollywood (WA) 6009
Holmesglen 3148
Holmesville 2286
Holmview 4207
Holsworthy Mil. P.O. 2173
Holt (ACT) 2615
Holt Rock 6355
Holwell 7251
Holyoake 6213
Home Hill 4806
Homebush (NSW) 2140
Homestead 4816
Homewood 3717
Hoopers Bridge 3464
Hope Valley (SA) 5090
Hope Valley (WA) 6165
Hopetoun (VIC) 3396
Hopetoun (WA) 6348
Hopetoun Gardens 3185
Hopevale (QLD) 4871
Hoppers Crossing 3030
Hordern Vale 3238
Hornsby 2077
Horseshoe Bay 4816
Horseshoe Bend 2320

Horsham 3400
Horsley Park 2164
Hotham Heights 3741
Hotham Hill 3051
Hotspur 3303
Houghton 5131
Houston 3128
Hove 5048
Hovea 6071
Howard 4659
Howard Springs 5791
Howden 7153
Howes Valley 2330
Howlong 2643
Howrah 7018
Howth 7316
Hoxton Park 2171
Hoyleton 5463
Hughenden 4821
Hughes (ACT) 2605
Hughesdale Via Carnegie 3163
Hughesdale Via Oakleigh 3166
Hume (ACT) 2620
Hume Weir (NSW) 3691
Humevale 3757
Humpty Doo 5791
Humula 2652
Hungerford 4493
Hunter 3560
Hunters Hill 2110
Hunterston 3971
Huntingdale (WA) 6110
Huntingdale Via Oakleigh (VIC) 3166
Huntingdale Via Oakleigh South (VIC) 3167
Huntingdon 2446
Huntley 2800
Huntleys Point 2111
Huntly 3551
Huon 3695
Huonville 7109
Hurlstone Park 2193
Hurstbridge 3099
Hurstville 2220
Hurstville South 2221
Huskisson 2540
Hyams Beach 2540
Hyde Park 5061
Hyden 6359
Hynam 5262

I

Icy Creek 3833
Ifield 2580
Iguana Creek 3866
Ilbilbie 4741
Ilford 2850
Ilfracombe 4727
Ilfraville 7251
Illabarook 3351
Illabo 2590
Illawarra (TAS) 7301
Illawarra (VIC) 3381
Illawong (Menai) 2234
Illowa 3282
Iluka (NSW) 2460
Iluka (WA) 6028
Imbil 4570
Inala 4077
Indented Head 3223
Indooroopilly 4068
Ingebyra 2627
Ingham 4850
Ingle Farm 5098
Ingleburn 2565
Ingleburn Mil. P.O. 2174
Inglehope 6213
Ingleside 2101
Inglewood (QLD) 4387
Inglewood (SA) 5133
Inglewood (VIC) 3517
Inglewood (WA) 6052
Injune 4454
Inman Valley 5211
Innaloo 6018
Innisfail 4860
Innot Hot Springs 4872
Interlaken 7120
Inverell 2360
Inveresk 7248
Invergordon 3636
Invergordon South 3634
Invergowrie 2350
Inverleigh 3321
Inverloch 3996
Invermay 7248
Iona (VIC) 3815
Ipswich 4305
Irish Town 7330
Iron Bank (SA) 5153
Iron Baron 5600
Iron Knob 5601
Ironside 4067
Irrewarra 3249
Irvinebank 4872
Irvingdale 4404
Irwin 6525
Irymple 3498
Isaacs (ACT) 2607
Isabella 2795
Isabella Plains (ACT) 2905
Isis Central Mill 4660
Isisford 4731
Isle Of Capri 4217
Islington 2296
Ivanhoe (NSW) 2878
Ivanhoe (VIC) 3079

J

Jabiru 5796
Jabuk 5301
Jacana Via Broadmeadows 3047
Jacana Via Glenroy 3046
Jackadgery 2461
Jackeys Marsh 7304
Jackson 4426
Jacobs Well (QLD) 4208
Jamberoo 2533
Jambin 4702
Jamboree Heights 4074
James Cook University Townsville 4811
Jamestown 5491
Jamieson 3723
Jamison Centre (ACT) 2614
Jancourt East 3266
Jandabup 6065
Jandakot 6164
Jandowae 4410
Jannali 2226
Jardee 6258
Jarklin 3517
Jarrah Glen 6398
Jarrahdale 6203
Jarrahmond 3888
Jarrahwood 6275
Jaspers Brush 2535
Jeeralang 3840
Jeetho 3945
Jembaicumbene 2622
Jennacubbine 6401
Jennings 4383
Jenolan Caves 2790
Jeogla 2350
Jeparit 3423
Jerangle 2630
Jericho (TAS) 7030
Jericho (QLD) 4702
Jerilderie 2716
Jerramungup 6337
Jerrys Plains 2330
Jerseyville 2431
Jervis Bay 2540
Jervois 5259
Jesmond 2299
Jetsonville 7254
Jilliby 2259
Jimboomba 4280
Jimbour 4352
Jimna 4515
Jindabyne 2627
Jindalee (QLD) 4074
Jindalee (WA) 6032
Jindera 2642
Jindivick 3818
Jingalup 6395
Jingellic 2642
Jingili (NT) 5792
Jitarning 6365
Johanna 3238
Johns River 2443
Johnsonville 3902
Jolimont (VIC) 3002
Jolimont (WA) 6014
Jondaryan 4403
Jones Hill 4570
Jones Island 2430
Joondalup 6027
Joondanna 6060
Jordanville Via Ashburton 3147
Jordanville Via Chadstone 3148
Joslin 5070
Joyner 4500
Judbury 7109
Judds Creek 2795
Jugiong 2726
Julatten 4880
Julia Creek 4823
Jumbuk 3869
Jumbunna 3951
Junction Hill 2460
Jundah 4736
Junee 2663
Jung 3399
Junortoun 3551
Jurien 6516

K

Kadina 5554
Kahibah 2290
Kaimkillenbun 4406
Kairi 4872
Kalamunda 6076
Kalang (NSW) 2454
Kalangadoo 5278
Kalannie 6468
Kalapa 4702
Kalbar 4309
Kalbarri 6536
Kaleen (ACT) 2617
Kalgoorlie 6430
Kalimna 3909
Kalinga 4030
Kalkallo 3064
Kallangur 4503
Kallaroo 6025
Kallista 3791
Kalorama 3766
Kalpowar 4630
Kamarah 2665
Kamarooka 3570
Kambah (ACT) 2902
Kambalda 6442
Kambalda West 6444
Kamona 7254
Kanahooka 2530
Kandanga 4570
Kandos 2848
Kangaloon 2576
Kangarilla 5157
Kangaroo Creek 2460
Kangaroo Flat (VIC) 3555
Kangaroo Ground 3097
Kangaroo Point (QLD) 4169
Kangaroo Point (Sylvania - NSW) 2224
Kangaroo Valley 2577
Kaniva 3419
Kanmantoo 5252
Kanumbra 3719
Kanwal 2259
Kanya 3381
Kaoota 7104
Kapooka Mil. P.O. 2661
Kapunda 5373
Karalee (QLD) 4306
Karama (NT) 5793
Karana Downs 4306
Karangi 2450
Karanja 7140
Karara 4352
Karawara 6152
Karawatha 4117
Kardella 3951
Kardinya 6163
Kareela 2232
Karingal 3199
Kariong 2251
Karkoo 5607
Karlgarin 6358
Karloo 6530
Karnak 3412
Karnup 6211
Karoola (TAS) 7254
Karoonda 5307
Karragarra Island 4165
Karragullen 6111
Karrakatta 6010
Karratha 6714
Karridale 6288
Karrinyup 6018
Kars Springs 2337
Karuah 2324
Karumba 4891
Katamatite 3649
Katandra 3634
Katandra North 3646
Katanning 6317
Katherine 5780
Katoomba 2780
Katunga 3640
Kawarren 3249
Kayena 7251
Kealba 3021
Kearney Springs 4350
Kearns 2558
Kearsley 2325
Kedron 4031
Keepit Dam 2340
Keilor 3036
Keilor Downs 3038
Keiraville 2500
Keith 5267
Keith Hall 2478
Kellatier 7325
Kellevie 7176
Kellyville 2153
Kelmscott 6111
Kelso (NSW) 2795
Kelso (QLD) 4815
Kelso (TAS) 7251
Kelvin 2380
Kelvin Grove 4059
Kembla Heights 2526
Kemblawarra 2505
Kemps Creek 2171
Kempsey 2440
Kempton 7030
Kendall 2439
Kendenup 6323
Kenebri 2396
Kenilworth 4574
Kenmare (VIC) 3395
Kenmore (NSW) 2580
Kenmore (QLD) 4069
Kennedys Creek 3239
Kennett River 3221
Kennington 3550
Kensington (NSW) 2033
Kensington (SA) 5068
Kensington (VIC) 3031
Kensington (WA) 6151
Kent Town 5067
Kentdale 6333
Kenthurst 2156
Kentish 7306
Kentlyn 2560
Kentucky 2354
Kenwick 6107
Keon Park Via Reservoir 3073
Keon Park Via Thomastown 3074
Keperra 4054
Kepnock 4670
Keppel Sands 4702
Kerang 3579
Kergunyah 3691
Kernot 3979
Kerrabee 2328
Kerrimuir 3129
Kerrisdale 3660
Kerrs Creek 2800
Kersbrook 5231
Keswick 5035
Kettering 7155
Kew (NSW) 2439
Kew (VIC) 3101
Kew East 3102
Kewdale 6105
Keyneton 5353
Keysborough 3173
Keysbrook 6206
Khancoban 2642
Ki Ki 5261
Kiah 2551
Kialla (VIC) 3631
Kialla East 3630
Kialla West 3613
Kiama 2533
Kiamal 3501
Kiandra 2630
Kiata 3418
Kidman Park 5025
Kidston 4871
Kielpa 5642
Kiewa 3691
Kilaben Bay 2283
Kilburn 5084
Kilcoy 4515
Kilcunda 3995
Kilkenny 5009
Kilkivan 4600
Killabakh Creek 2429
Killara (NSW) 2071
Killarney (QLD) 4373
Killarney (VIC) 3282
Killarney Heights 2087
Killarney Vale 2261
Killcare 2256
Killiecrankie 7255
Killingworth (NSW) 2301
Killora 7156
Kilmany 3851
Kilmore 3764
Kilsyth 3137
Kimba 5641
Kimberley 7304
Kimbriki 2429
Kin Kin 4571
Kinchela Creek 2440
Kincumber 2250
Kincumber South 2256
Kindred 7310
King Island 7256
King Parrot Creek 3658
King River 6330
King Valley 3678
Kingaroy 4610
Kinglake 3763
Kinglake Central 3757

Kinglake West 3757
Kingoonya 5710
Kings Cross 2011
Kings Langley 2147
Kings Meadows 7249
Kings Park (SA) 5034
Kingsbury 3083
Kingscliff 2487
Kingscote 5223
Kingsdale 2580
Kingsdene 2118
Kingsford 2032
Kingsgrove 2208
Kingsholme 4208
Kingsley 6026
Kingsthorpe 4400
Kingston (ACT) 2604
Kingston (QLD) 4114
Kingston (TAS) 7150
Kingston (VIC) 3364
Kingston Beach 7151
Kingston Park 5049
Kingston SE (SA) 5275
Kingston-On-Murray 5331
Kingstown 2358
Kingsvale 2587
Kingsville South Via Newport 3015
Kingsville South Via Yarraville 3013
Kingsville Via Footscray West 3012
Kingsville Via Yarraville 3013
Kingsway West 2208
Kingswood (NSW) 2750
Kingswood (SA) 5062
Kingswood Park 2750
Kinimakatka 3418
Kinkora 4680
Kinkuna 3130
Kinnabulla 3483
Kioloa 2539
Kippa-Ring 4020
Kippax Centre (ACT) 2615
Kirkstall 3282
Kirra 4225
Kirrawee 2232
Kirribilli 2061
Kirup 6251
Kirwan 4814
Kitchener 2325
Kithbrook 3666
Kleinig 6722
Kleinton 4352
Klemzig 5087
Knorrit Flat 2424
Knowsley 3551
Knoxfield 3180
Koallah 3257
Koetong 3704
Kogan 4406
Kogarah 2217
Kojaneerup 6328
Kojonup 6395
Kolan South 4670
Koloona 2403
Kolora 3265
Kondinin 6367
Kondut 6605
Kongorong 5291
Kongwak 3951
Konnongorring 6603
Koojan 6510
Koolan Island 6733
Koolewong 2256
Kooloonong 3597
Koolunga 5464
Koolyanobbing 6427
Koombana 6722
Koomeela 7254
Koonawarra (NSW) 2530
Koonda 3669
Koondoola 6064
Koondrook 3580
Koongal 4701
Koongamia 6056
Koonwarra 3954
Koonya (TAS) 7187
Kooragang Island 2304
Koorainghat 2430
Koorawatha 2807
Koorda 6475
Kooreh 3478
Kooreh South 3465
Kooringal (NSW) 2650
Kooringal (QLD) 4025
Koorlong 3501
Koornalla 3844
Kooroocheang 3364
Kooroongarra 4357
Kootingal 2352
Kooweerup 3981
Kooyong Via Hawthorn 3122
Kooyong Via Malvern 3144
Kooyong Via Toorak 3142
Koraleigh 2739
Korbel 6415
Koriella 3714
Korobeit 3341
Koroit 3282
Korong Vale 3520
Kororo 2450
Korrelocking 6485
Korumburra 3950
Korweinguboora 3461
Kotara 2289
Kotara East 2305
Kotara Fair 2289
Kotta 3565
Kotupna 3638
Koumala 4738
Kowanyama 4871
Koyuga 3622
Koyuga South 3621
Krambach 2429
Krambruk North 3233
Kronkup 6330
Krowera 3945
Kudla (SA) 5115
Kukerin 6352
Kulikup 6244
Kulin 6365
Kulja 6470
Kulnura 2250
Kulpi 4352
Kulwin 3490
Kumarina 6642
Kumbia 4610
Kundabung 2441
Kunghur 2484
Kununoppin 6489
Kununurra 6743
Kunyung 3930
Kuraby 4112
Kuranda 4872
Kurmond 2757
Kurnell 2231
Kurraba Point 2089
Kurrajong 2758
Kurralta Park 5037
Kurri Kurri 2327
Kurrimine Beach 4871
Kurting 3517
Kurunjang 3337
Kurwongbah 4503
Kuttabul 4741
Kweda 6306
Kwinana 6167
Kwolyin 6385
Kyabram 3620
Kyalite 2739
Kyancutta 5651
Kybunga 5463
Kybybolite 5262
Kyeemagh 2216
Kyle Bay 2221
Kyneton 3444
Kynuna 4823
Kyogle 2474

L

La Perouse 2036
Laanecoorie 3463
Laang 3265
Labertouche 3816
Labrador 4215
Laburnum 3130
Laceys Creek 4521
Lachlan 7140
Lackrana 7255
Lady Barron 7255
Ladysmith 2652
Laggan 2583
Lagoons 7215
Laguna 2325
Lah 3393
Laharum 3401
Laheys Creek 2852
Laidley 4341
Lajamanu 5780
Lake Albert 2650
Lake Bathurst 2580
Lake Biddy 6355
Lake Boga 3584
Lake Bolac 3351
Lake Cargelligo 2672
Lake Cathie 2445
Lake Charm 3581
Lake Conjola 2539
Lake Crescent 7120
Lake Grace 6353
Lake Heights 2502
Lake Illawarra 2528
Lake King 6356
Lake Leake 7210
Lake Mackenzie 7304
Lake Margaret 7467
Lake Mundi 3312
Lake Munmorah 2259
Lake Rowan 3727
Lake St Clair 7140
Lake Tyers 3887
Lake Tyers Beach 3909
Lake View 5520
Lake Wyangan 2680
Lakemba 2195
Lakemba South 2209
Lakes Entrance 3909
Lal Lal 3357
Lalbert 3542
Lalla 7254
Lalor 3075
Lalor Park 2147
Lamb Island 4165
Lambton 2299
Lameroo 5302
Lancaster 3620
Lancefield 3435
Lancefield Junction 3430
Lancelin 6044
Landsborough (QLD) 4550
Landsborough (VIC) 3384
Lane Cove 2066
Lanena 7251
Lang Lang 3984
Langford 6155
Langhorne Creek 5255
Langkoop 3312
Langley 3444
Langley Vale 2426
Langwarrin 3910
Lansdowne 2430
Lansvale 2166
Lapoinya 7325
Lapstone 2773
Lara 3212
Largs 2320
Largs Bay 5016
Largs North 5016
Larpent 3249
Larrakeyah (NT) 5790
Larrapinta 4110
Larras Lee 2866
Larrimah 5780
Lascelles 3487
Latham (ACT) 2615
Latham (WA) 6616
Lathlain 6100
Latimer 4211
Latrobe 7307
Latrobe University 3083
Lauderdale 7021
Laughtondale 2255
Launceston 7250
Launceston South 7249
Launching Place 3139
Laura (QLD) 4871
Laura (SA) 5480
Laurel Hill 2649
Laurieton 2443
Lauriston 3444
Lavender Bay 2060
Lavers Hill 3238
Laverton (VIC) 3028
Laverton (WA) 6440
Laverton North 3026
Laverton RAAF (VIC) 3027
Lavington 2641
Lawaluk 3329
Lawes 4345
Lawnton 4501
Lawrence (NSW) 2460
Lawson 2783
Le Roy 3844
Leabrook 5068
Leaconfield 2335
Leadville 2831
Leanyer (NT) 5793
Learmonth (WA) 6707
Learmonth (VIC) 3352
Leawarra (NSW) 2160
Leawood Gardens 5150
Lebrina 7254
Leda 6170
Ledge Point 6043
Lee Point (NT) 5792
Leebrooke 3862
Leederville 6007
Leeman 6514
Leeming 6155
Leeton 2705
Leeville 2470
Lefroy 7252
Legana 7251
Legerwood 7254
Legume 2476
Legunia 7254
Leichardt (VIC) 3516
Leichhardt 4305
Leichhardt (NSW) 2040
Leigh Creek (VIC) 3352
Leigh Creek (SA) 5731
Leightonfield 2163
Leinster 6437
Leitchville 3567
Leith 7315
Lemana Junction 7304
Lemnos 3631
Lemon Springs 3419
Lemon Tree Passage 2301
Lemont 7120
Lemonthyme 7306
Lenah Valley 7008
Leneva 3691
Lennox Head 2478
Lenswood 5240
Leonards Hill 3461
Leonay 2750
Leongatha 3953
Leonora 6438
Leopold 3224
Leppington 2171
Leslie Vale 7100
Lesmurdie 6076
Lethbridge (VIC) 3332
Lethbridge Park (NSW) 2770
Leumeah 2560
Leura 2780
Levendale 7120
Lewisham (NSW) 2049
Lewisham (TAS) 7173
Lexton 3352
Leyburn 4352
Liapootah 7140
Licola 3858
Lidcombe 2141
Liddell 2333
Lidsdale 2790
Lidster 2800
Liena 7304
Lietinna 7254
Liffey 7301
Lightning Ridge 2834
Lileah 7330
Lilli Pilli 2229
Lillico (TAS) 7310
Lillimur 3415
Lillimur South 3419
Lilydale (TAS) 7254
Lilydale (VIC) 3140
Lilyfield 2040
Lima 3673
Limbri 2352
Limeburners Creek 2324
Limerick 2583
Limevale 4384
Lincolnville 3033
Linda 7466
Lindeman Island 4741
Linden 2778
Linden Park 5065
Lindenow 3865
Lindenow South 3866
Lindfield 2070
Lindisfarne 7015
Lindsay View 2474
Lindum 4178
Linga 3509
Linley Point 2066
Linley Valley 6558
Linton 3360
Linville 4306
Lipson 5607
Lisarow 2251
Lisle 7254
Lismore (NSW) 2480
Lismore (VIC) 3324
Liston 2372
Litchfield 3480
Lithgow 2790
Little Bay 2036
Little Grove 6330
Little Hampton 3458
Little Hartley 2790
Little Plain 2360
Little River (VIC) 3211
Little Swanport 7190
Littlehampton 5250
Littleton 2790
Liverpool 2170
Liverpool Mil. P.O. 2172
Llandaff 7190
Llandilo 2760
Llanelly 3551
Llangothlin 2365
Llanherne 7170
Llewellyn 7213
Lobethal 5241
Loccota 7255
Loch 3945
Loch Sport 3851
Lochiel (SA) 5510
Lochinvar 2321
Lock 5633
Lockhart 2656
Lockhart River 4871
Lockington 3563
Lockleys 5032
Lockridge 6054
Locksley (NSW) 2795
Locksley (VIC) 3665
Lockwood 3551
Lockyer (QLD) 4344
Lockyer (WA) 6330
Loftus 2232
Logan 3475
Logan Reserve 4133
Loganholme 4129
Loganlea 4204
Londonderry 2753
Lone Pine (VIC) 3691
Long Flat 2446
Long Gully 3550
Long Island (QLD) 4741
Long Jetty 2261
Longford (TAS) 7301
Longford (VIC) 3851
Longlea (VIC) 3551
Longley (TAS) 7103
Longley Lower 7105
Longreach 4730
Longueville 2066
Longwarry 3816
Longwarry East 3818
Longwarry South 3818
Longwood (SA) 5153
Longwood (VIC) 3665
Lonnavale 7109
Lonsdale 5160
Loongana 7315
Lord Howe Island 2898
Lorinna 7306
Lorne (NSW) 2439
Lorne (VIC) 3232
Lorquon 3418
Lostock 2311
Lota 4179
Lottah 7254
Louisville 7190
Louth 2840
Louth Bay (SA) 5607
Loveday 5345
Lovely Banks 3221
Lovett Bay 2105
Low Head 7252
Lowanna 2450
Lowbank 5320
Lowden 6240
Lowdina 7026
Lower Acacia Creek 2372
Lower Bucca 2450
Lower Chittering 6084
Lower Creek 2440
Lower Gellibrand 3237
Lower Hawkesbury 2255
Lower Kalgan 6330
Lower King 6330
Lower Light 5501
Lower Mangrove 2251
Lower Marshes 7030
Lower Mitcham 5062
Lower Norton Creek 3401
Lower Plenty 3093

Lower Portland 2756
Lower Templestowe 3107
Lowesdale 2646
Lowmead 4676
Lowood 4311
Lowther 2790
Loxton 5333
Loyetea 7316
Lubeck 3381
Lucas Heights 2234
Lucaston 7107
Lucinda 4850
Lucindale 5272
Lucknow (NSW) 2800
Lucknow (VIC) 3875
Luddenham 2750
Ludlow 6271
Ludmilla (NT) 5790
Lue 2850
Lugarno 2210
Lughrata 7255
Luina 7321
Lunawanna 7161
Lune River 7116
Lurg 3672
Lurline Bay 2035
Lurnea 2170
Luscombe 4207
Lutana 7009
Lutwyche 4030
Lyalls Mill 6225
Lyetta 7251
Lymington 7112
Lymwood 7256
Lynchford 7467
Lynchs Creek 2474
Lyndhurst (SA) 5731
Lyndhurst (NSW) 2797
Lyndoch 5351
Lyneham (ACT) 2602
Lynton (SA) 5062
Lynwood 6155
Lyons (ACT) 2606
Lyons (VIC) 3304
Lyonville 3461
Lyra 4352
Lyrup 5343
Lysterfield 3156
Lytton 4178

M

Ma Ma Creek 4347
Maatsuyker Island 7001
Macalister 4406
Macarthur (ACT) 2904
Macarthur (VIC) 3286
Macclesfield (SA) 5153
Macclesfield (VIC) 3782
Macdonald Park 5121
Macedon 3440
Macgregor (ACT) 2615
Macgregor (QLD) 4109
Machans Beach 4871
Mackay 4740
MacKenzie 4156
Mackintosh 3564
Macknade 4850
Macks Creek 3971
Macksville 2447
Maclagan 4352
Maclean 2463
Macleay Island 4165
Macleod 3085
Macmasters Beach 2250
Macorna 3578
Macorna North 3568
Macquarie (ACT) 2614
Macquarie Centre 2113
Macquarie Fields 2564
Macquarie Island 7150
Macquarie Plains 7140
Macquarie Settlement 7301
Macquarie University (North Ryde) 2109
Macrossan 4816
Madalya 3971
Madarinah 6722
Maddington 6109
Madora 6211
Maffra (VIC) 3860
Maffra West Upper 3859
Magill 5072
Magpie 3352
Magra 7140
Mahogany Creek 6072
Mahomets Flats 6530
Maianbar 2230
Maida Vale 6057
Maiden Gully 3551
Maidenwell 4315
Maidstone 3012
Mailors Flat 3282
Main Beach 4217
Main Ridge 3928
Maindample 3721
Maitland (NSW) 2320
Maitland (SA) 5573
Majorca 3465
Majors Creek 2622
Majura (ACT) 2609
Malabar 2036
Malaga 6062
Malak (NT) 5793
Malanda 4885
Malbina 7140
Maldon (NSW) 2571
Maldon (VIC) 3463
Maleny 4552
Mallacoota 3889
Mallala 5502
Mallan 3586
Mallanganee 2470
Malmsbury 3446
Malones 3282
Malua Bay 2536
Malvern (SA) 5061
Malvern (VIC) 3144
Mambray Creek 5495
Manahan 2200
Manangatang 3546
Mandagery 2870
Mandalong 2264
Mandogalup 6167
Mandurah 6210
Mandurama 2792
Mandurang 3551
Mangalore (TAS) 7030
Mangalore (VIC) 3663
Mangana 7214
Mangerton 2500
Mango Hill 4503
Mangoplah 2652
Mangrove Mountain 2250
Maniana 6107
Manifold 3218
Manildra 2865
Manilla 2346
Maningrida 5791
Manjimup 6258
Manly (NSW) 2095
Manly (QLD) 4179
Manly Vale 2093
Manly West 4179
Manmanning 6465
Mannahill 5440
Mannerim 3222
Mannering Park 2259
Manningham 5086
Mannum 5238
Mannus 2653
Manoora (SA) 5414
Manor 3030
Mansfield (QLD) 4122
Mansfield (VIC) 3722
Mansfield Park 5012
Mantung 5308
Manuka (ACT) 2603
Manunda 4870
Manyana 2539
Manypeaks (WA) 6328
Mapleton 4560
Marama 5307
Maranboy 5780
Marangaroo 6064
Maraylya 2765
Marayong 2148
Marble Bar 6760
Marburg 4346
March 2800
Marcoola 4564
Marcus Hill 3222
Mardella 6204
Marden 5070
Mareeba 4880
Margaret River 6285
Margate (TAS) 7153
Margate (QLD) 4019
Maria Island 7190
Marian 4741
Maribyrnong 3032
Mariginiup 6065
Marino 5049
Marion 5043
Marion Bay 7175
Marionba 7175
Market Square (Geelong) 3220
Marks Point 2280
Markwell 2423
Markwood 3678
Marla 5724
Marlborough 4705
Marlee 2429
Marleston 5033
Marlo 3888
Marmion 6020
Marmong Point 2284
Marnoo 3387
Marom Creek 2480
Marong 3515
Maroochydore 4558
Maroona 3290
Maroota 2756
Maroubra 2035
Marrabel 5413
Marradong 6391
Marrangaroo 2790
Marrar 2652
Marrara (NT) 5793
Marrawah 7330
Marree 5733
Marrickville 2204
Marryatville 5068
Marsden 4203
Marsden Park 2765
Marsfield 2122
Marshall 3216
Marshdale 2420
Martins Creek (VIC) 3888
Martinsville 2265
Martynvale 4870
Marulan 2579
Marungi 3634
Marvel Loch 6426
Mary Farms 4871
Maryborough (QLD) 4650
Maryborough (VIC) 3465
Marybrook 6282
Maryfields 2560
Maryknoll 3812
Marysville (VIC) 3779
Maryvale (NSW) 2820
Maryvale (QLD) 4370
Maryville (NSW) 2293
Mascot 2020
Mascot Airport 2020
Maslin Beach 5170
Mataranka 5780
Matcham 2250
Mater Hill 4101
Mater Misericordiae Hospital 2065
Matheson (NSW) 2370
Mathiesons (VIC) 3612
Mathinna 7214
Mathoura 2710
Matlock 3723
Matong 2652
Matraville 2036
Maude (NSW) 2711
Maudsland 4210
Mawbanna 7321
Mawson (ACT) 2607
Mawson (Antarctica) 7150
Mawson (WA) 6302
Maxwelton 4816
Maya 6614
Mayanup 6244
Mayberry 7304
Maydena 7140
Mayfield (TAS) 7248
Mayfield (NSW) 2304
Maylands (SA) 5069
Maylands (WA) 6051
Mayne 4006
Mayrung 2710
Mays Hill 2145
McAlinden 6225
McCallums Hill 2195
McCrae 3938
McCullys Gap 2333
McDowall 4053
McGraths Hill 2756
McKees Hill 2480
McKellar (ACT) 2617
McKenzie Creek 3401
McKillop 3796
McKinlay 4823
McKinnon 3204
McLaren Flat 5171
McLaren Vale 5171
McMahons Creek 3799
McMahons Point 2060
Meadow Creek 3678
Meadow Flat 2795
Meadowbank (NSW) 2114
Meadowbanks 7140
Meadows 5201
Meandarra 4422
Meander 7304
Meatian 3585
Meckering 6405
Medina 6167
Medindie 5081
Medlow Bath 2780
Medowie 2301
Meeandah 4008
Meekatharra 6642
Meeniyan 3956
Meerlieu 3862
Meerschaum Vale 2477
Megalong 2785
Megan 2453
Melba (ACT) 2615
MELBOURNE
CITY 3000
GPO PRIVATE BOXES 3001
Melbourne (Queens Road) 3004
Melbourne (St Kilda Road) 3004
Melbourne East 3002
Melbourne International Airport 3045
Melbourne University 3052
Mella 7330
Melrose (SA) 5483
Melrose (TAS) 7310
Melrose Park 2114
Melton 3337
Melton Mowbray 7030
Melton South 3338
Melville (Erskine Park - NSW) 2759
Melville (WA) 6156
Melville Forest 3315
Melwood 3875
Memana 7255
Mena Creek 4871
Menai 2234
Menangle 2568
Menangle Park 2563
Mendooran 2842
Mengha 7330
Menindee (NSW) 2879
Meningie (SA) 5264
Menora 6050
Mentone 3194
Menzies (WA) 6436
Mepunga 3268
Merah North 2385
Merbein 3505
Mercunda 5308
Meredith 3333
Merewether 2291
Merlbah 5333
Merimbula 2548
Merinda 4805
Meringandan 4352
Meringur 3496
Merino 3310
Merlynston 3058
Mermaid Beach 4218
Mernda 3754
Meroo Meadow 2540
Merredin 6415
Merri 3068
Merri View 3280
Merricks 3916
Merricks North 3926
Merrigum 3618
Merrijig 3723
Merrimac 4226
Merriton 5523
Merriwa (NSW) 2329
Merriwa (WA) 6030
Merriwagga 2652
Merrygoen 2831
Merrylands 2160
Merrywinebone 2387
Mersey Lea 7305
Merton (TAS) 7010
Merton (VIC) 3715
Metcalfe 3448
Metcalfe East 3444
Metford 2323
Metricup 6282
Mettler 6328
Metung 3904
Meunna 7325
Mia Mia 3444
Miami 4220
Miandetta 2825
Michelago 2620
Mickleham 3064
Mid Valley 3840
Middle Cove 2068
Middle Creek Rail 3375
Middle Head 2088
Middle Park (QLD) 4074
Middle Park (VIC) 3206
Middle Ridge 4350
Middle Swan 6056
Middlemount 4746
Middleton (SA) 5213
Middleton (TAS) 7163
Middleton Beach 6330
Midland 6056
Midvale 6056
Midway Point 7171
Miena 7030
Miga Lake 3401
Mil Lel 5291
Mila 2632
Milabeena 7325
Milang 5256
Milawa 3678
Milbrulong 2656
Mildura (VIC) 3500
Mile End (SA) 5031
Miles 4415
Miling 6575
Mill Park 3082
Millaa Millaa 4886
Millbank 2440
Millbrook (NSW) 2500
Millbrook (VIC) 3352
Millendon 6056
Miller 2168
Millers Forest 2324
Millfield 2325
Millgrove 3799
Millicent 5280
Millingimbi 5791
Millmerran 4357
Millner (NT) 5792
Milloo 3572
Millswood 5034

Millthorpe 2798
Milltown (VIC) 3304
Milparinka 2880
Milperra 2214
Milperra Bridge 2170
Milsons Passage 2253
Milsons Point 2061
Milton (NSW) 2538
Milton (QLD) 4064
Milton Centre 4064
Milvale 2594
Mincha 3575
Mincha East 3567
Mindarie (SA) 5309
Mindarie (WA) 6030
Miners Rest 3352
Minerva 3218
Mingela 4816
Mingenew 6522
Minhamite 3287
Minimay 3413
Mininera 3351
Minjah 3280
Minlaton 5575
Minmi 2287
Minnamurra 2532
Minnipa 5654
Minnivale 6462
Mintable Opal Fields (SA) 5724
Mintaro 5415
Minto (NSW) 2566
Minyama 4575
Minyip 3392
Mira Mar 6330
Miram 3415
Miranda 2228
Mirani 4754
Mirannie 2330
Mirboo 3871
Mirboo East 3870
Mirboo North 3871
Mirboo South 3956
Miriam Vale 4677
Miriwinni 4871
Mirra View 2264
Mirrabooka (WA) 6061
Mirrimbah 3722
Mirrool 2665
Missabotti 2449
Missenden Road 2050
Mission Beach 4854
Mitcham (SA) 5062
Mitcham (VIC) 3132
Mitchell (ACT) 2911
Mitchell (QLD) 4465
Mitchell Park (SA) 5043
Mitchells Flat 2330
Mitchells Island 2430
Mitchelton 4053
Mitiamo 3573
Mitre 3410
Mitta Mitta 3701
Mittagong 2575
Mittyack 3533
Moama (NSW) 2739
Moana (SA) 5169
Moculta 5353
Modbury 5092
Model Farms 2153
Modewarre 3240
Moe 3825
Moffat Beach 4551
Moggill 4070
Mogo 2536
Mogriguy 2830
Mogumber 6506
Moil (NT) 5792
Moina 7306
Moira 2710
Mole Creek 7304
Molendinar 4214
Molesworth (TAS) 7140
Molesworth (VIC) 3718
Moleton 2450
Moliagul 3472
Mollerin 6471
Mollongghip 3352
Mollymook 2539
Molong 2866
Moltema 7304
Molyullah 3673
Mona Vale (NSW) 2103
Mona Vale (TAS) 7209
Monak 2739
Monaro Crescent (ACT) 2603
Monarto South 5254
Monash (ACT) 2904
Monash (SA) 5342
Monash Park 2111
Monash University 3168
Monbulk 3793
Mondure 4611
Monegeetta 3433
Monegeetta North 3434
Monga 2622
Mongarlowe 2622
Monkerai 2415
Monkland 4570
Monomeith 3984
Mont Albert Via Box Hill North 3129
Mont Albert Via Surrey Hills 3127
Mont Park 3085
Montacute (TAS) 7140
Montacute (SA) 5134
Montagu 7330
Montagu Bay 7018
Montague 3205
Montana 7304
Monteagle 2594
Montefiores 2820
Montello 7320
Monterey 2217
Montmorency 3094
Monto 4630
Montrose (TAS) 7010
Montrose (VIC) 3765
Montumana 7321
Montville 4560
Mooball 2483
Moogara 7140
Moolap 3221
Mooloolaba 4557
Mooloolah 4553
Moomba Park 3060
Moombooldool 2665
Moonah 7009
Moonambel 3478
Moonan Brook 2337
Moonan Flat 2337
Moonbi 2352
Moondarra 3825
Moonee Beach 2450
Moonee Ponds 3039
Moonee Vale 3055
Mooney Mooney 2254
Moonie 4406
Moonies Hill 6320
Moonta 5558
Moonyoonooka 6532
Moora (WA) 6510
Moorabbin 3189
Moorabbin Airport Via Cheltenham 3192
Moorabbin Airport Via Mentone 3194
Moorak 5291
Mooral Creek 2429
Mooralla 3408
Moore 4306
Moorebank 2170
Moores Pocket 4305
Moorina 7254
Moorine Rock 6425
Moorland (NSW) 2443
Moorlands (SA) 5301
Moorleah 7325
Moorleigh (VIC) 3167
Moormbool West 3523
Moorook (SA) 5332
Moorooka (QLD) 4105
Mooroolbark 3138
Mooroopna 3629
Moranbah 4744
Morang South 3752
Morans Crossing 2550
Morawa 6623
Morayfield 4506
Morchard 5486
Mordialloc 3195
Moreland East 3057
Moreland Via Brunswick 3056
Moreland Via Brunswick East 3057
Moreland Via Brunswick West 3055
Moreland Via Coburg 3058
Moreland West 3055
Morella 4730
Moresby (WA) 6530
Morgan 5320
Morgiana 3301
Moriac 3240
Moriarty 7307
Morisset 2264
Morkalla 3496
Morley 6062
Morningside 4170
Mornington (WA) 6221
Mornington (TAS) 7018
Mornington (VIC) 3931
Morpeth 2321
Morphett Vale 5162
Morphettville 5043
Morrells Hill 3870
Morrison 3334
Mortdale 2223
Mortlake (NSW) 2137
Mortlake (VIC) 3272
Morundah 2700
Moruya 2537
Morven (NSW) 2660
Morven (QLD) 4468
Morwell 3840
Morwell River Prison 3870
Mosman 2088
Mosman Park 6012
Mosmans Bay 2088
Moss Vale 2577
Mossgiel 2878
Mossiface 3885
Mossman (QLD) 4873
Mossy Point 2537
Moulamein 2739
Moulden (NT) 5787
Moulyinning 6315
Mount Alfred 3691
Mount Austin 2650
Mount Barker (SA) 5251
Mount Barker (WA) 6324
Mount Barrow 7257
Mount Beauty 3699
Mount Best 3960
Mount Bryan 5418
Mount Buffalo Chalet 3745
Mount Buller 3723
Mount Burnett 3781
Mount Burr 5279
Mount Camel 3523
Mount Cameron 3370
Mount Christian 4741
Mount Claremont 6010
Mount Clear 3350
Mount Colah 2079
Mount Cole 3377
Mount Compass 5210
Mount Coolon 4804
Mount Cotton 4163
Mount Cottrell 3030
Mount Crosby 4306
Mount Dandenong 3767
Mount David 2795
Mount Direction 7252
Mount Druitt 2770
Mount Duneed (VIC) 3216
Mount Egerton 3345
Mount Eliza 3930
Mount Evelyn 3796
Mount Field 7140
Mount Franklin 3461
Mount Gambier 5290
Mount Gambier Private Bags 5291
Mount Garnet 4872
Mount George 2424
Mount Glorious 4520
Mount Gravatt 4122
Mount Hawthorn 6016
Mount Helen 3350
Mount Helena 6555
Mount Hicks 7325
Mount Hope 2877
Mount Horeb 2729
Mount Hotham 3741
Mount Hutton 2290
Mount Isa 4825
Mount Jeffcott 3525
Mount Keira 2500
Mount Kembla 2526
Mount Kokeby 6304
Mount Kuring-Gai 2080
Mount Kynoch 4352
Mount Larcom 4695
Mount Lawley 6050
Mount Lewis 2200
Mount Lloyd 7140
Mount Lofty 4350
Mount Lonarch 3468
Mount Macedon 3441
Mount Madden 6356
Mount Magnet 6638
Mount Martha 3934
Mount Mee 4521
Mount Molloy 4880
Mount Morgan 4714
Mount Moriac 3240
Mount Nathan 4211
Mount Nebo 4520
Mount Nelson 7007
Mount Nicholas 7215
Mount Olive 2330
Mount Ommaney 4074
Mount Osmond 5064
Mount Ossa 4741
Mount Ousley 2519
Mount Pelion 4741
Mount Perry 4671
Mount Pleasant (Dayboro-QLD) 4521
Mount Pleasant (Mackay-QLD) 4740
Mount Pleasant (SA) 5235
Mount Pleasant (VIC) 3350
Mount Pleasant (WA) 6153
Mount Pritchard 2170
Mount Prospect 3364
Mount Richmond 3306
Mount Riverview 2774
Mount Rowan 3352
Mount Rumney 7170
Mount Russell 2360
Mount Samson 4520
Mount Seymour 7120
Mount St Thomas 2500
Mount Stromlo (ACT) 2611
Mount Stuart 7000
Mount Surprise 4871
Mount Sylvia 4343
Mount Tamborine 4272
Mount Tarcoola 6530
Mount Taylor 3875
Mount Torrens 5244
Mount Tyson 4356
Mount Victoria 2786
Mount View 2325
Mount Wallace 3342
Mount Warren Park 4207
Mount Warrigal 2528
Mount Waverley 3149
Mount Wedge 5670
Mount White 2250
Mount Wilson 2786
Mountain Gate 3156
Mountain River 7106
Moura 4718
Mourilyan 4858
Mourquong 2648
Moutajup 3294
Mowbray 7248
Moyhu 3732
Moyston 3377
Muchea 6501
Muckadilla 4461
Muckleford 3451
Muckleford South 3462
Mudamuckla 5685
Mudgee 2850
Mudgeeraba 4213
Mudgegonga 3737
Mudjimba 4564
Mukinbudin 6479
Mulbring 2323
Mulgildie 4630
Mulgoa 2750
Mulgrave (NSW) 2756
Mulgrave (VIC) 3170
Mulgrave North 3170
Mullaley 2379
Mullaloo 6025
Mullalyup 6252
Mullengandra 2644
Mullengudgery 2825
Mullewa 6630
Mullins 3700
Mullion Creek 2800
Mullumbimby 2482
Mulwala 2647
Mumballup 6225
Mumbannar 3304
Mumbil 2820
Mummulgum 2470
Mundaring 6073
Mundijong 6202
Mundingburra 4812
Mundiwindi 6753
Mundoora 5520
Mundubbera 4626
Mundulla 5270
Mungallala 4467
Mungindi 2406
Munno Para 5115
Munro 3863
Munster 6166
Muntadgin 6420
Muradup 6394
Murarrie 4172
Murchison 3610
Murdinga (SA) 5607
Murdoch (VIC) 3677
Murdoch (WA) 6150
Murdunna 7178
Muresk 6401
Murga 2864
Murgheboluc 3221
Murgon 4605
Murmungee 3747
Muronbung 2830
Murphys Creek (QLD) 4352
Murphys Creek (VIC) 3551
Murrabit 3579
Murrami 2705
Murray Bridge 5253
Murray Bridge Private Bags 5254
Murray Town 5481
Murraydale 3586
Murrayville 3512
Murrindal 3885
Murrindindi 3717
Murringo 2586
Murrumba Downs 4503
Murrumbateman 2582
Murrumbeena 3163
Murrumburrah 2587
Murrungower Lower 3888
Murrurundi 2338
Murtoa 3390
Murwillumbah 2484
Muscle Creek 2333
Musk 3461
Muskvale 3461
Musselboro 7212
Muswellbrook 2333
Mutarnee 4816
Mutchilba 4872
Muttaburra 4732
Muttama 2722
Myall (NSW) 2423
Myalla 7325
Myamyn 3304
Myaree 6154
Myers Creek 3777
Myers Flat 3556
Myleston 2454
Mylor 5153
Mypolonga 5254
Myponga 5202
Myrniong 3341
Myrrhee 3732
Myrtle Bank (SA) 5064
Myrtle Bank (TAS) 7257
Myrtlebank 3851
Myrtleford 3737
Mysia 3536
Mystic Park 3581

N

Nabageena 7330
Nabawa 6532
Nabiac 2312
Nabowla 7254
Nagambie 3608
Nailsworth 5083
Nairne 5252
Nakara (NT) 5792
Nala 7120
Nalangil 3249
Nalkain 6485
Nambour 4560
Nambrok 3847
Nambucca Heads 2448
Nana Glen 2450
Nanango 4315
Nandaly 3533
Nanga Brook 6218
Nangiloc 3494
Nangus 2722
Nangwarry 5277
Nanneella 3561
Nannup 6275

Nantawarra 5550
Napier 6330
Napoleons 3352
Nar Nar Goon 3812
Naracoopa 7256
Naracoorte 5271
Naradhan 2669
Naraling 6532
Narangba 4504
Narara 2250
Narbethong 3778
Nareen 3315
Narellan 2567
Narembeen 6369
Naremburn 2065
Nariel Creek 3705
Naringal 3277
Naringaningalook East 3636
Naroghid 3266
Narooma 2546
Narrabeen 2101
Narrabri 2390
Narrabundah (ACT) 2604
Narrandera 2700
Narrawa (TAS) 7310
Narrawallee 2539
Narraweena 2099
Narrawong 3285
Narre Warren 3805
Narre Warren East 3804
Narre Warren North 3804
Narrikup 6326
Narrogin 6312
Narromine 2821
Narrung (SA) 5259
Narrung (VIC) 3597
Narwee 2209
Nashdale 2800
Nashua 2479
Nathalia 3638
Nathan 4111
Natimuk 3409
National Park 7140
Natone 7321
Nattai 2570
Natte Yallock 3465
Natural Bridge 4211
Natya 3597
Naval Base 6165
Naval PO Balmoral 2091
Naval PO Nowra 2540
Navarre 3384
Navigators 3357
Nayook 3821
Nebo 4742
Nedlands West 6009
Needilup 6336
Needles 7304
Neerabup 6031
Neerim 3831
Neerim Junction 3821
Neerim North 3821
Neerina 7153
Neika 7102
Neilborough 3570
Neilrex 2831
Nelia 4816
Nelligen 2536
Nelly Bay 4816
Nelson (NSW) 2765
Nelson (VIC) 3292
Nelson Bay 2315
Nelsons Hill 3136
Nemingha 2340
Nerang 4211
Neranwood 4213
Neridup 6450
Nerrena 3953
Nerrena East 3956
Nerriga 2622
Nerrigundah 2545
Nerrin Nerrin 3351
Nerrina 3350
Netherby (SA) 5062
Netherby (VIC) 3418
Nethercote 2549
Netley 5037
Neuarpurr 3413
Neurea 2820
Neutral Bay 2089
Nevertire 2831
Neville 2799
New Angledool 2832
New Berrima 2577
New Brighton 2483
New Farm 4005
New Gisborne 3438
New Lambton 2305
New Mollyann 2842
New Norcia 6509
New Norfolk 7140
New Town (TAS) 7008
New Well 5357
Newborough 3825
Newbridge (NSW) 2795
Newbridge (VIC) 3551
Newburn 6104
Newbury 3458
Newcastle 2300
Newcastle University 2308
Newcastle Waters 5760
Newcastle West 2302
Newcomb 3219
Newdegate 6355
Newell 4873
Newfield 3268
Newham 3442
Newhaven 3925
Newington 3350
Newlands Estate 3058
Newlyn 3364
Newman 6753
Newmarket (QLD) 4051
Newmarket (VIC) 3031
Newmerella 3886
Newnham 7248
Newport (VIC) 3015
Newport Beach 2106
Newry 3859
Newrybar 2479
Newstead (QLD) 4006
Newstead (TAS) 7250
Newstead (VIC) 3462
Newton (SA) 5074
Newton Boyd 2370
Newtown 4305
Newtown (Geelong) 3220
Newtown (NSW) 2042
Ngulu (Bathurst Island) 5791
Ngukurr 5780
Nhill 3418
Nhulunbuy 5797
Ni Ni East 3417
Niagara Park 2250
Niangala 2354
Nicholls Rivulet 7112
Nichols Point 3501
Nicholson 3882
Niddrie 3042
Nietta 7315
Nightcliff 5792
Nikenbah 4655
Nildottie 5238
Nile 7212
Nilma 3821
Nimbin 2480
Nimmitabel 2631
Ninda 3533
Ningi 4511
Nirranda 3268
Noarlunga Centre 5168
Noarlunga Downs 5168
Nobby 4360
Nobby Beach 4218
Noble Park 3174
Noggerup 6225
Nokaning 6415
Nollamara 6061
Nonning 5710
Noojee 3833
Nook 7306
Noonamah 5791
Noonbinna 2794
Noongaar 6424
Noorat 3265
Noorinbee 3889
Noosa Heads 4567
Noosaville 4566
Noradjuha 3401
Norah Head 2263
Noranda 6062
Noraville 2263
Nords Wharf 2301
Norfolk Island 2899
Norlane 3214
Norman Park 4170
Normanhurst 2076
Normanton 4890
Normanville (SA) 5204
Nornalup 6333
Norong 3682
Norseman 6443
North Adelaide 5006
North Baandee 6413
North Balwyn 3104
North Beach (WA) 6020
North Carlton 3054
North Dandalup 6207
North Essendon 3041
North Fitzroy 3068
North Fremantle 6159
North Haven (NSW) 2443
North Haven (SA) 5018
North Head 2095
North Heidelberg 3081
North Hobart Private Boxes 7002
North Kew Via Kew 3101
North Kew Via Stradbroke Park 3102
North Lake 6163
North Melbourne 3051
North Motton 7315
North Parramatta 2151
North Perth 6006
North Plympton 5037
North Richmond 2754
North Rocks 2151
North Ryde 2113
North Shields 5607
North Shore (VIC) 3214
North Star 2408
North Steyne 2095
North Strathfield 2137
North Sydney 2060
North Tamborine 4272
North Ward 4810
Northam 6401
Northampton 6535
Northbridge (WA) 6000
Northbridge (NSW) 2063
Northcliffe 6262
Northcote 3070
Northdown 7307
Northfield 5085
Northgate (QLD) 4013
Northland Centre (Preston VIC) 3072
Northlands 4350
Northmead 2152
Northwood (NSW) 2066
Norton Summit 5136
Norwell 4208
Norwood (SA) 5067
Norwood Avenue 7250
Notley Hills 7251
Novar Gardens 5040
Nowa Nowa 3887
Nowendoc 2354
Nowergup 6032
Nowingi 3494
Nowra 2541
Nubeena 7184
Nudgee 4014
Nugent 7172
Nukarni 6480
Nulkaba 2325
Nullagine 6758
Nullamanna 2360
Nullawarre 3268
Nullawil 3529
Numbaa 2540
Number One 2424
Numbla Vale 2628
Numbulwar (NT) 5780
Numeralla 2630
Numinbah Valley 4211
Numulgi 2480
Numurkah 3636
Nunamara 7257
Nunawading 3131
Nundah (QLD) 4012
Nundle 2340
Nungarin 6490
Nunjikompita 5685
Nunyle 6566
Nuriootpa 5355
Nurrabiel 3401
Nutfield 3099
Nyabing 6341
Nyah 3594
Nyah West 3595
Nyamup 6258
Nyarrin 3533
Nymagee 2831
Nymboida 2460
Nyngan 2825
Nyora 3987

O

O.B. Flat 5291
O'Connor (ACT) 2601
O'Connor (WA) 6163
O'Sullivan Beach (SA) 5166
Oak Flats 2529
Oak Park 3046
Oakbank 5243
Oakdale 2570
Oakey 4401
Oaklands 2646
Oaklands Junction 3047
Oaklands Park 5046
Oakleigh 3166
Oakleigh South 3167
Oaks 7303
Oakville 2765
Oakwood (TAS) 7182
Oatlands 7120
Oatley 2223
Oberon 2787
Ocean Beach 2257
Ocean Grove 3226
Ocean Reef 6027
Ocean View 4521
Oenpelli 5791
Officer 3809
Ogmore 4706
Ohalloran Hill 5158
Olary 5440
Old Bar 2430
Old Beach 7017
Old Bonalbo 2470
Old Erowal Bay 2540
Old Guildford 2161
Old Junee 2652
Old Koreelah 2476
Old Noarlunga 5168
Old Toongabbie 2146
Oldina 7325
Olinda 3788
Olympic Dam (SA) 5725
Omanama 4352
Omeo 3898
Ondit 3249
One Mile Beach (Forster) 2428
One Tree Hill (SA) 5114
Ongerup 6336
Onslow 6710
Oodnadatta 5734
Oonah 7321
Oonoonba 4811
Oorindi 4816
Ootha 2797
Opossum Bay 7023
Ora Banda 6431
Orange 2800
Orange Grove (WA) 6109
Orangeville 2570
Oranmeir 2622
Orbost 3888
Orchard Hills 2748
Orelia 6167
Orford (TAS) 7190
Orford (VIC) 3301
Orielton 7172
Orient Point 2540
Ormeau 4208
Ormiston 4163
Ormley 7214
Ormond Via Bentleigh 3204
Ormond Via Bentleigh East 3165
Ormond Via Carnegie 3163
Ormond Via Caulfield South 3162
Orroroo 5431
Osborne (SA) 5017
Osborne Park (WA) 6017
Osborns Flat 3691
Osmaston 7303
Osmington 6285
Osterley 7140
Otago 7017
Otford 2508
Ottoway 5013
Ourimbah 2258
Ouse 7140
Outer Harbor 5018
Outtrim 3951
Ouyen 3490
Ovens 3738
Ovingham 5082
Owen 5460
Owens Gap 2337
Oxenford 4210
Oxford Falls 2100
Oxford Park 4053
Oxley (Hay) 2711
Oxley (NSW) 2903
Oxley (QLD) 4075
Oxley (VIC) 3678
Oxley Park 2760
Oxley Vale 2340
Oyster Bay (NSW) 2225
Oyster Cove (TAS) 7100
Ozenkadnook 3413

P

Paaratte 3268
Pacific Fair 4218
Pacific Palms 2428
Padbury 6025
Paddington (NSW) 2021
Paddington (QLD) 4064
Padstow 2211
Padthaway 5271
Page (ACT) 2614
Pagewood 2035
Paisley Park 3025
Pakenham 3810
Palana 7255
Palgarup 6258
Palinyewah 2648
Pallamallawa 2399
Pallara 4110
Pallarenda 4810
Palm Beach (NSW) 2108
Palm Beach (QLD) 4221
Palm Cove 4871
Palm Grove 2258
Palm Island 4816
Palm Vale 2484
Palmer 5237
Palmers Island 2460
Palmerston 5787
Palmwoods (QLD) 4555
Palmyra 6157
Paloona 7310
Paluma 4816
Pambula 2549
Panania 2213
Panitya East 3490
Panmure 3265
Pannawonica 6716
Panorama 5041
Pantapin 6384
Panton Hill 3759
Paper Beach 7251
Pappinbarra 2446
Para Hills 5096
Para Vista 5093
Paraburdoo 6754
Parachilna 5730
Paracombe 5132
Paradise (TAS) 7306
Paradise (SA) 5075
Paradise Beach (VIC) 3851
Paradise Island 4217
Paradise Point 4216
Paradise Waters 4217
Parafield 5107
Parafield Airport 5106
Paralowie 5108
Parangana 7306
Parap 5790
Parattah 7120
Pardelup 6324
Parilla 5303
Paringa 5340
Paringi 3500
Park Avenue 4701
Park Holme 5043
Park Orchards 3114
Park Ridge 4125
Parkdale Via Mentone 3194
Parkdale Via Mordialloc 3195
Parkers Corner 3825
Parkerville 6553
Parkes (ACT) 2600
Parkes (NSW) 2870
Parkeston 6434
Parkham 7304
Parkhurst 4702
Parkinson 4115
Parklands 7320
Parklea 2148
Parkmore 3131
Parkside (Ayr - QLD) 4807
Parkside (Mt Isa - QLD) 4825
Parkside (SA) 5063
Parkville (NSW) 2337
Parkville (VIC) 3052
Parliament House (Melbourne) 3002
Parliament House (Perth WA) 6000
Parliament House (Sydney) 2000
Parmelia 6167
Parndana 5220
Parrakie 5301
Parramatta 2150
Parramatta Park (QLD) 4870
Parrearra 4575
Parryville 6333
Paruna 5311
Parwan 3340
Pasadena 5042
Pascoe Vale 3044
Paskeville 5552
Pastoria East 3444
Patchewollock 3491
Pateena 7301
Paterson 2421
Patersonia 7257
Patho 3564
Patonga 2256
Patterson 3189
Patterson Lakes 3197
Paulls Valley 6076
Pawleena 7172
Pawtella 7120
Pax Hill 3844
Paxton 2325
Paynedale 6239
Payneham 5070
Paynes Crossing 2325
Paynes Find 6612
Paynesville (VIC) 3880
Peak Crossing 4306
Peak Hill 2869
Peak View 2630
Peake 5301
Peakhurst 2210
Pearce (ACT) 2607
Pearce RAAF (WA) 6085
Pearcedale 3912
Pearl Beach 2256
Pearshape 7256
Peats Ridge 2250
Pederick 3620
Peebinga 5307
Peechelba 3678
Peel 2795
Peel Island 4163
Peelwood 2583
Pegarah 7256
Pegs Creek 6714
Pekina 5487
Pelaw Main 2327
Pelham 7030
Pelican Flat 2281
Pelican Island 2440
Pelton 2325
Pelverata 7104
Pemberton 6260
Pembrooke 2446
Pender 3071
Pendle Hill 2145
Penfield 5121
Penguin 7316
Penna 7171
Pennant Hills 2120
Penneshaw 5222
Pennington 5013
Pennydale 3192
Penola 5277
Penong 5690
Penrith 2750
Penrose 2579
Penshurst (NSW) 2222
Penshurst (VIC) 3289
Pentland 4816
Peppermint Grove 6011
Peranga 4352
Peregian Beach 4573
Perenjori 6620
Perillup 6324
Perisher Valley 2630
Peronne 3413
Perponda 5308
Perth (TAS) 7300

PERTH (WA)
CITY 6000
GPO PRIVATE BOXES 6001

Perth Airport 6105
Perthville 2795
Petcheys Bay 7112
Peterborough (SA) 5422
Peterborough (VIC) 3270
Peterhead 5016
Petersham 2049
Petersons 3658
Petrie 4502
Petrie Terrace 4000
Petworth 5125
Pheasant Creek 3757
Pheasants Nest 2574
Phegans Bay 2256
Phillip (ACT) 2606
Phillip Bay 2036
Pialba 4655
Pialligo (ACT) 2609
Piangil 3597
Piavella 3572
Piawaning 6572
Piccadilly 5151
Pickering Brook 6076
Picnic Bay 4816
Picnic Point (NSW) 2213
Picola 3639
Picton (NSW) 2571
Picton (WA) 6229
Pier Millan 3533
Piersons Point 7152
Piesse Brook 6076
Piesseville 6315
Pillar Valley 2462
Pilliga 2388
Pimlico 2478
Pimpama 4209
Pimpinio 3401
Pindari Dam 2361
Pindi Pindi 4741
Pindimar 2324
Pine Creek 5782
Pine Lodge South 3631
Pine Mountain 4306
Pine Point 5571
Pine Ridge (Quirindi) 2343
Pine Ridge (Leadville) 2831
Pines Forest 3200
Pinewood 3149
Pingaring 6357
Pingelly 6308
Pingrup 6343
Pinjar 6065
Pinjarra 6208
Pinjarra Hills 4069
Pinkenba 4008
Pinklands 4163
Pinnacle 4741
Pinnaroo 5304
Pioneer (Ayr - QLD) 4807
Pioneer (Mt Isa - QLD) 4825
Pioneer (TAS) 7254
Point Leo 3916
Pipe Clay Bay 7253
Pipers Brook 7254
Pipers Creek 3444
Pipers Flat 2847
Pipers River 7252
Pira 3585
Pirron Yallock 3249
Pithara 6608
Pitt Town 2756
Pittsworth 4356
Pleasant Hills 2658
Pleasure Point 2171
Plenty (TAS) 7140
Plenty (VIC) 3090
Pleystowe 4741
Plumpton (NSW) 2761
Plympton (SA) 5038
Plympton North 5037
Poatina 7302
Point Clare 2250
Point Cook RAAF 3029
Point Leo 3916
Point Lonsdale 3225
Point Lookout 4184
Point Pearce 5573
Point Piper 2027
Point Vernon 4655
Pokataroo 2833
Pokolbin 2320
Police Point 7116
Polkemmet 3401
Pomborneit 3257
Pomona (NSW) 2648
Pomona (QLD) 4568
Pomonal 3381
Pontville 7030
Poochera 5655
Poolaijelo 3312
Pooncarie 2648
Pooraka 5095
Pootilla 3352
Poowong 3988
Popanyinning 6309
Porepunkah 3740
Porongurup 6324
Port Adelaide 5015
Port Albert 3971
Port Arthur 7182
Port Augusta 5700
Port Augusta Private Bags 5710
Port Botany 2036
Port Broughton 5522
Port Campbell 3269
Port Clinton 5570
Port Davey 7170
Port Denison 6525
Port Douglas 4871
Port Elliot 5212
Port Fairy 3284
Port Franklin 3964
Port Germein 5495
Port Hacking 2229
Port Hedland 6721
Port Hughes 5558
Port Huon 7115
Port Kembla 2505
Port Kenny 5671
Port Latta 7320
Port Lincoln 5606
Port Lincoln Private Bags 5607
Port Macdonnell 5291
Port Macquarie 2444
Port Melbourne 3207
Port Neill 5604
Port Noarlunga 5167
Port Pirie 5540
Port Sorell 7307
Port Victoria 5573
Port Vincent 5581
Port Wakefield 5550
Port Welshpool 3965
Port Willunga 5173
Portarlington 3223
Porters Retreat 2787
Portland (NSW) 2847
Portland (VIC) 3305
Portsea 3944
Postans 6167
Potts Hill 2143
Potts Point 2011
Pottsville Beach 2489
Powelltown 3797
Powers Creek 3312
Powranna 7300
Pozieres 4352
Prahran 3181
Prairie (QLD) 4816
Prairie (VIC) 3572
Prairiewood 2176
Premaydena 7185
Premer 2381
Prentice North 3685
Preolenna 7325
Preservation Bay 7316
Preston (TAS) 7315
Preston (VIC) 3072
Prestons (NSW) 2170
Pretty Beach 2256
Price 5570
Priestdale 4217
Primbee 2504
Primrose Sands 7173
Prince Henry Heights 4350
Prince Of Wales Bay 7009
Princess Alexandra Hospital 4102
Princess River 7466
Princetown 3269
Priory 7216
Proctors 3962
Proserpine 4800
Prospect (NSW) 2149
Prospect (SA) 5082
Prospect Vale 7250
Proston 4613
Puckapunyal Mil. P.O. 3662
Pularumpi (NT) 5791
Pullabooka 2810
Pullenvale 4069
Punchbowl (TAS) 7249
Punchbowl (NSW) 2196
Pura Pura 3271
Puralka 3311
Purfleet 2430
Purlewaugh 2357
Purnim 3279
Purrumbete North 3260
Purrumbete South 3256
Putney 2112
Putty 2330
Pyalong 3521
Pyengana 7254
Pyes Creek 2372
Pymble 2073
Pyramid Hill 3575
Pyree 2540
Pyrmont 2009
Pyrton 6055

Q

Quaama 2550
Quairading 6383
Quakers Hill 2763
Quakers Hill R.A.N.A.T.E. 2764
Qualen 6302
Qualeup 6395
Quambatook 3540
Quambone 2831
Quamby Brook 7304
Quandialla 2721
Quantong 3405
Quarry Hill 3550
Queanbeyan 2620
Queen Victoria Terrace PO (ACT) 2600
Queens Beach 4805
Queens Park 6107
Queens Road - Melbourne 3004
Queenscliff (NSW) 2096
Queenscliff (VIC) 3225
Queenstown (SA) 5014
Queenstown (TAS) 7467
Quellington 6302
Quilpie 4480
Quindalup 6281
Quindanning 6391
Quinninup 6258
Quinns Rocks 6030
Quipolly 2343
Quirindi 2343
Quoiba 7310
Quorn 5433
Quorrobolong 2325

R

Raby 2566
Raby Bay 4163
Raceview 4305
Radnor 7182
Raglan (NSW) 2795
Raglan (QLD) 4697
Railton 7305
Railway Estate 4810
Rainbow 3424
Rainbow Bay 4225
Rainbow Beach 4570
Rainbow Pacific 2445
Rainworth 4065
Raleigh 2454
Ralphs Bay 7021
Ramco 5322
Raminea 7116
Ramsgate 2217
Rand 2642
Randalls Bay 7112
Randwick 2031
Ranelagh 7109
Raneleigh 3930
Ranga 7255
Rangeview (VIC) 3132
Rangeville 4350
Rangeway 6530
Rankin Park 2287
Rankins Springs 2669
Ransome 4154
Rapid Bay 5204
Rapid Creek (NT) 5792
Rappville 2470
Rasmussen 4815
Rathdowney 4287
Rathmines 2283
Rathscar 3465

Ravensbourne 4352
Ravensdale 7190
Ravenshoe 4872
Ravensthorpe 6346
Ravenswood (QLD) 4816
Ravenswood (TAS) 7250
Ravenswood (VIC) 3551
Ravensworth 2330
Rawdon Island 2446
Rawdon Vale 2422
Rawlinna 6434
Rawson 3825
Raymond Island 3880
Raymond Terrace 2324
Raymonds Hill 4305
Raywood 3570
Red Bluff 3695
Red Cliffs (VIC) 3496
Red Hill (ACT) 2603
Red Hill (QLD) 4059
Red Hill (VIC) 3937
Red Hill (WA) 6056
Red Hills (TAS) 7304
Red Range 2370
Red Rock 2456
Redan 3350
Redbank (QLD) 4301
Redbank (VIC) 3478
Redcliffe (QLD) 4020
Redcliffe (WA) 6104
Redesdale 3444
Redfern 2016
Redhead 2290
Redhill (SA) 5521
Redland Bay 4165
Redlynch 4872
Redmond 6327
Redpa 7330
Redwood Park 5097
Reedy Creek (QLD) 4228
Reedy Creek (VIC) 3658
Reedy Marsh 7304
Reefton (NSW) 2666
Reekara 7256
Regatta Point 7468
Regency Park 5010
Regent Via Preston 3072
Regent Via Reservoir 3073
Regents Park 2143
Regentville 2750
Reid (ACT) 2601
Reid (WA) 6434
Reids Flat 2586
Reidsdale 2622
Rekuna 7026
Relbia 7250
Remlaw 3401
Rendelsham 5280
Renison Bell 7469
Renmark 5341
Rennie 2646
Renown Park 5008
Repton 2454
Research 3095
Reservoir 3073
Retreat 7254
Revesby 2212
Reynella 5161
Rheban 7190
Rheola 3517
Rhodes 2138
Rhyll 3923
Rhyndaston 7120
Riana 7316
Richardson (ACT) 2905
Richlands (QLD) 4077
Richmond (NSW) 2753
Richmond (QLD) 4822
Richmond (SA) 5033
Richmond (TAS) 7025
Richmond (VIC) 3121
Richmond Hill (TAS) 7251
Richmond RAAF (NSW) 2755
Riddell 3431
Riddells Creek 3431
Ridgehaven 5097
Ridgeway (TAS) 7101
Ridgley 7321
Ridleyton 5008
Rileys Hill 2472
Ringarooma 7254
Ringwood (VIC) 3134
Ringwood East 3135
Ripley 4306
Ripplebrook 3818
Ripponhurst 3286
Ripponlea Via Balaclava 3183
Ripponlea Via Elsternwick 3185
Risdon Park 5540
Risdon Vale 7016
River Hills 4074
Riverford 3862
Riverside (TAS) 7250
Riverstone 2765
Riverton (SA) 5412
Riverton (WA) 6155
Rivervale 6103
Riverview (NSW) 2066
Riverview (QLD) 4303
Riverwood 2210
Rivett (ACT) 2611
Roadvale 4310
Robbins Island 7330
Robe 5276
Robertson (NSW) 2577
Robertson (QLD) 4109
Robertstown 5381
Robigana 7251
Robina 4226
Robinson (VIC) 3019
Robinvale 3549
Rochedale 4123
Rocherlea 7248
Roches Beach 7021
Rochester 3561
Rochford 3442
Rock Flat 2630
Rock Valley (NSW) 2480
Rockbank 3335
Rockdale 2216
Rockhampton 4700
Rockhampton Forward 4702
Rockhampton Mc Private Boxes 4702
Rockhampton North 4701
Rockingham 6168
Rockingham Beach 6168
Rocklands 3401
Rocklea (QLD) 4106
Rockley (NSW) 2795
Rocklyn 3364
Rockville 4350
Rocky Cape 7321
Rocky Glen 2357
Rocky Gully 6397
Rocky Hall 2550
Rodd Point 2046
Roebourne 6718
Roelands 6226
Roger River 7330
Rokeby (TAS) 7019
Rokeby (VIC) 3821
Rokewood 3330
Rokewood Junction 3351
Roland 7306
Roleystone 6111
Rollands Plains 2441
Rolleston 4702
Rollingstone 4816
Roma 4455
Romaine Heights 7320
Romsey 3434
Rooty Hill 2766
Rosa Brook 6285
Rosa Glen 6285
Rosalie 4064
Rosamel 6230
Rosanna 3084
Rose Bay (NSW) 2029
Rose Bay (TAS) 7015
Rose Bay North 2030
Rose Park 5067
Rosebank 2480
Rosebery (NSW) 2018
Rosebery (NT) 5786
Rosebery (TAS) 7470
Rosebery (VIC) 3395
Rosebrook (VIC) 3285
Rosebud 3939
Rosebud West 3940
Rosedale (QLD) 4674
Rosedale (VIC) 3847
Rosegarland 7140
Rosehill 2142
Roselands 2196
Roselea 2118
Rosella 4741
Rosemeadow 2560
Roses Tier 7212
Rosetta 7010
Rosevale (TAS) 7257
Rosevears 7251
Roseville 2069
Rosewater 5013
Rosewater East 5013
Rosewood (QLD) 4340
Rosewood (Wagga Wagga - NSW) 2652
Roseworthy 5371
Roslyn 2580
Roslynmeade 3564
Rosny 7018
Ross 7209
Ross Creek 3351
Rossarden 7213
Rosslyn Park 5072
Rossmore 2171
Rossmoyne 6155
Rostrevor (SA) 5073
Rothwell 4020
Roto 2675
Rottnest Island 6161
Rouchel Brook 2336
Round Corner 2158
Rous 2477
Rous Mill 2477
Rouse Hill 2153
Rowallan 7306
Rowella 7251
Rowena 2387
Rowland Flat 5352
Rowsley 3340
Rowville 3178
Roxby Downs 5725
Roy Hill 6753
Royal Brisbane Hospital 4029
Royal George 7213
Royal Melb Hospital 3050
Royal North Shore Hospital 2065
Royal Park (SA) 5014
Royal Womens Hospital 3053
Royalla 2620
Roys 3869
Royston Park 5070
Rozelle 2039
Ruabon 6282
Rubicon 3712
Ruby 3953
Rubyvale 4702
Rudall 5642
Ruffy 3666
Rufus River 2648
Rugby 2583
Rukenvale 2474
Runaway Bay 4216
Runcorn 4113
Running Stream 2850
Runnymede 7190
Rupanyup 3388
Ruse 2560
Rushcutters Bay 2011
Rushworth 3612
Rushy Lagoon 7254
Russell 2600
Russell Island 4165
Russell Lea 2046
Russell Vale 2517
Rutherford 2320
Rutherglen 3685
Ruthven (NSW) 2480
Rutland 7030
Rydal 2790
Rydalmere 2116
Ryde 2112
Ryde East 2113
Rye 3941
Rye Park 2586
Rylstone 2849

S

Sackville North 2756
Saddleworth 5413
Sadleir 2168
Sadliers Crossing 4305
Safety Bay (WA) 6169
Safety Beach (VIC) 3936
Sagar Place 2113
Sailors Falls 3461
Salamander Bay 2301
Sale 3850
Salisbury (NSW) 2420
Salisbury (QLD) 4107
Salisbury (SA) 5108
Salisbury (VIC) 3418
Salisbury East 5109
Salisbury Heights 5109
Salisbury Park 5109
Salisbury Plain (SA) 5109
Salisbury West 3517
Salmon Gums 6445
Salt Ash 2301
Saltwater River 7186
Samford 4520
Samson 6163
Samsonvale 4523
San Remo 2262
San Remo (VIC) 3925
Sanctuary Point 2540
Sandalwood 5309
Sanderson 5793
Sanderston 5237
Sandfly 7104
Sandford (TAS) 7020
Sandford (VIC) 3312
Sandgate (NSW) 2304
Sandgate (QLD) 4017
Sandhill 7249
Sandhurst 3550
Sandon 3462
Sandown Village 3171
Sandringham (NSW) 2219
Sandringham (VIC) 3191
Sandstone 6639
Sandy Bay 7005
Sandy Creek (SA) 5350
Sandy Creek (VIC) 3695
Sandy Flat 2372
Sandy Hollow 2333
Sandy Point (Liverpool - NSW) 2171
Sandy Point (VIC) 3959
Sans Souci (NSW) 2219
Santa Teresa 5751
Sapphire (QLD) 4702
Saratoga 2250
Sardine Creek 3888
Sarina 4737
Sarina Beach 4737
Sarsfield 3883
Sassafras (TAS) 7307
Sassafras (VIC) 3787
Sassafras South 3791
Saunders Beach 4816
Savage River 7321
Savernake 2646
Sawtell 2452
Sawyers Valley 6074
Scaddan 6447
Scamander 7215
Scarborough 2515
Scarborough (QLD) 4020
Scarborough (WA) 6019
Scarness 4656
Scarsdale 3351
Scheyville 2756
Schofields 2762
Scone 2337
Scoresby 3179
Scotland Island 2105
Scotsburn 3357
Scott Creek (SA) 5153
Scotts Creek (VIC) 3267
Scotts Head 2447
Scottsdale 7254
Scullin (ACT) 2614
Sea Lake 3533
Seabrook 7322
Seacliff 5049
Seacombe Gardens 5047
Seacombe Heights 5047
Seaford (SA) 5169
Seaford (VIC) 3198
Seaforth (NSW) 2092
Seaforth (QLD) 4741
Seaham 2324
Seaholme 3018
Seal Rocks 2423
Seaspray 3851
Seaton (SA) 5023
Seaton (VIC) 3858
Seaview Downs 5049
Sebastian 3556
Sebastopol (NSW) 2666
Sebastopol (VIC) 3356
Second Valley 5204
Sedan 5353
Seddon Via Footscray 3011
Seddon Via Yarraville 3013
Sedgwick 3551
Seelands 2460
Sefton 2162
Sefton Park (SA) 5083
Segenhoe 2337
Selbourne 7257
Selby 3159
Sellheim 4816
Sellicks Beach 5174
Sellicks Hill (SA) 5174
Semaphore 5019
Serpentine (VIC) 3517
Serpentine (WA) 6205

Serviceton 3420
Seven Creeks 3666
Seven Hills (NSW) 2147
Seven Hills (QLD) 4170
Seven Mile Beach 7170
Seventeen Mile Rocks 4073
Severnlea 4352
Seville 3139
Seymour (TAS) 7215
Seymour (VIC) 3660
Shackleton 6386
Shailer Park 4128
Shandeen 3218
Shanes Park 2760
Shannon 7030
Shannon River Mill 6258
Shannon Vale (VIC) 3898
Shark Bay 6537
Sharks Point 7171
Sharon 4670
Shay Gap 6761
Sheas Creek 2044
Sheep Hills 3401
Sheffield 7306
Sheidow Park 5158
Shelbourne 3463
Shelbourne East 3551
Sheldon 4157
Shelford 3329
Shelley 3701
Shelley (WA) 6155
Shellharbour 2529
Shelly Beach (NSW) 2261
Shelly Beach 7190
Shenton Park 6008
Shepherds Flat 3461
Shepparton 3630
Shepparton East 3631
Sherbrooke 3789
Sheridan Heights 2161
Sheringa 5607
Sherlock 5301
Sherwood (QLD) 4075
Sherwood Hills 2560
Shipwrights Point 7115
Shoal Bay 2315
Shoalhaven Heads 2535
Shoalwater 6169
Shooters Hill 2787
Shoreham 3916
Shorewell 7320
Shorncliffe 4017
Shortland 2307
Shotts 6225
Shute Harbour 4802
Siding Springs (NSW) 2357
Sidmouth 7251
Sidonia 3444
Siesta Park 6282
Silkwood 4856
Silkwood East 4857
Silvan 3795
Silverdale 2750
Silverton 2880
Silverwater (Lidcombe) 2141
Silverwater Via Morisett 2264
Simmie 3622
Simpson 3266
Simpson's Bay 7158
Simpsons Creek 3888
Singleton (NSW) 2330
Singleton (WA) 6211
Singleton Mil Po 2331
Sisters Creek 7325
Skenes Creek 3233
Skipton 3361
Skye 5072
Slacks Creek 4127
Slade Point 4740
Sladen 3220
Slopen Main Beach 7186
Smeaton 3364
Smiggin Holes 2630
Smithfield (NSW) 2164
Smithfield (QLD) 4871
Smithfield (SA) 5114
Smiths Gully 3760
Smithton (TAS) 7330
Smithtown (NSW) 2440
Smoky Bay 5680
Smythes Creek 3351
Smythesdale 3351
Snake Valley 3351
Snowtown 5520
Snug 7154
Sodwalls 2790
Sofala 2795
Soldiers Hill 4825
Soldiers Point 2301
Solomontown 5540
Solway 3147
Somers 3927
Somersby 2250
Somerset 7322
Somerset Dam 4312
Somerset Hill 6333
Somerton (NSW) 2340
Somerton (VIC) 3062
Somerton Park (SA) 5044
Somerville 3912
Sorell 7172
Sorell Creek 7140
Sorlie 2086
Sorrento 4217
Sorrento (VIC) 3943
Sorrento (WA) 6020
South Arm 7022
South Brisbane 4101
South Fremantle 6162
South Golden Beach Via New Brighton (NSW) 2483
South Grafton 2461
South Hedland 6722
South Johnstone 4859
South Kilkerran 5573
South Kumminin 6368
South Melbourne 3205
South Molle 4741
South Mount Cameron 7254
South Perth 6151
South West Rocks 2431
South Yarra 3141
Southbrook 4352
Southend 5280
Southern Cross (VIC) 3282
Southern Cross (WA) 6426
Southern River 6110
Southland Centre (Cheltenham) 3192
Southport (QLD) 4215
Southport (TAS) 7116
Southtown 4350
Sovereign Hill 3350
Spalding (SA) 5454
Spalding (WA) 6530
Spalford 7315
Spargo Creek 3461
Spearwood 6163
Spectacle Island 2000
Speed 3488
Speers Point 2284
Speewa (NSW) 2739
Speewa (VIC) 3585
Spence (ACT) 2615
Spencer 2255
Spencer Park 6330
Spencers Brook 6401
Spicers Creek 2820
Spinifex 3597
Spion Kop 2327
Spit Junction 2088
Spotswood 3015
Sprent 7315
Spreyton 7310
Spring Bay 7190
Spring Beach 7190
Spring Bluff 4352
Spring Gardens 3280
Spring Grove 2470
Spring Gully 3550
Spring Hill 7030
Spring Hill (NSW) 2800
Spring Hill (QLD) 4004
Spring Hill (VIC) 3444
Spring Plains 3444
Spring Ridge 2343
Spring Terrace 2798
Springbank 3352
Springbrook 4213
Springdale 2666
Springfield (Moonah) 7009
Springfield (NSW) 2250
Springfield (SA) 5062
Springfield (TAS) 7254
Springhill 4004
Springhurst 3682
Springmount 3364
Springsure 4722
Springton 5235
Springvale (VIC) 3171
Springvale South 3172
Springwood (NSW) 2777
Springwood (QLD) 4127
St Agnes 5097
St Albans (NSW) 2255
St Albans (VIC) 3021
St Andrews (NSW) 2566
St Andrews (VIC) 3761
St Arnaud 3478
St Clair (NSW) 2759
St Evins 3317
St George (QLD) 4487
St Georges (SA) 5064
St Georges Basin 2540
St Helena 3088
St Helens (VIC) 3285
St Helens (TAS) 7216
St Helens Park 2560
St Huberts Island 2256
St Ives 2075
St James (VIC) 3727
St James (WA) 6102
St Johns Park 2176
St Johns Wood 4060
St Kilda 5110
St Kilda (VIC) 3182
St Kilda Road - Melbourne 3004
St Lawrence 4707
St Leonards (NSW) 2065
St Leonards (VIC) 3223
St Leonards (TAS) 7250
St Lucia (QLD) 4067
St Marys (NSW) 2760
St Marys (SA) 5042
St Marys (TAS) 7215
St Morris 5068
St Pauls 2031
St Peters (NSW) 2044
St Peters Pass 7120
St Peters (SA) 5069
St Vincents Hosp 3065
Stafford 4053
Staghorn Flat 3691
Stamford 4821
Stanford Merthyr 2327
Stanhope (NSW) 2335
Stanhope (VIC) 3623
Stanley (TAS) 7331
Stanley (VIC) 3747
Stanmore 2048
Stannifer 2369
Stannum 2371
Stansbury 5582
Stanthorpe 4380
Stanwell 4702
Stanwell Park 2508
Stanwell Tops 2508
Stapylton 4207
Staughton Vale 3221
Stavely 3291
Staverton 7306
Stawell 3380
Steels Creek 3775
Steiglitz (QLD) 4207
Steiglitz (VIC) 3331
Steiglitz (TAS) 7216
Stenhouse Bay 5577
Stephens 4227
Stepney 5069
Steppes 7030
Stewart (VIC) 3496
Stewarts Bay 7182
Stewarts Brook 2337
Stirling (ACT) 2611
Stirling (SA) 5152
Stirling (WA) 6021
Stirling North 5710
Stockdale 3862
Stockinbingal 2725
Stockport 5410
Stockton 2295
Stockwell 5355
Stokers Siding 2484
Stokes Point 2107
Stonehaven 3221
Stonehenge (TAS) 7120
Stonehenge (QLD) 4730
Stones Corner 4120
Stoneville 6554
Stoneyford 3256
Stonor 7120
Stony Creek 3957
Stonyfell 5066
Stoodley 7306
Store Creek 2820
Stormlea 7184
Storys Creek 7213
Stotts Creek 2487
Stove Hill 6714
Stowport 7321
Stradbroke 3851
Stradbroke Park 3102
Strahan 7468
Strangways 3461
Stratford (NSW) 2422
Stratford (QLD) 4872
Stratford (VIC) 3862
Strath Creek 3658
Strathalbyn 5255
Strathallan 3622
Strathblane 7116
Strathbogie (VIC) 3666
Strathbogie North 3669
Strathdownie 3312
Strathfield 2135
Strathfield South 2136
Strathfield West 2140
Strathfieldsaye 3551
Strathgordon 7140
Strathkellar 3301
Strathlea 3364
Strathmerton 3641
Strathmore (Boort) 3537
Strathmore (Essendon North) 3041
Strathpine 4500
Strawberry Hills 2012
Streaky Bay 5680
Streatham 3351
Stretton 4116
Strickland 7140
Stringer Creek 7321
Stroud 2425
Stroud Road 2415
Stuart 4811
Stuart Mill 3478
Stuart Park (NT) 5790
Stuart Town 2820
Stuarts Point 2441
Studfield 3152
Sturt 5047
Subiaco 6008
Success 6164
Suffolk Park 2481
Sulphur Creek 7316
Summer Hill 2130
Summerdale 7250
Summerfield 3570
Summerhill 7250
Summerland Point 2259
Summers 3564
Summertown 5141
Sumner (QLD) 4074
Sumner (VIC) 3057
Sunbury 3429
Sundale 4215
Sunny Corner 2795
Sunnybank 4109
Sunnycliffs 3496
Sunnyside (NSW) 2372
Sunnyside (TAS) 7305
Sunset (QLD) 4825
Sunset Beach 6530
Sunshine (NSW) 2324
Sunshine (VIC) 3020
Sunshine Beach 4567
Surat 4417
Surfers Paradise 4217
Surges Bay 7116
Surrey Downs 5126
Surrey Farm 5127
Surrey Hills (VIC) 3127
Surry Hills (NSW) 2010
Sussex Inlet 2540
Sutherland (NSW) 2232
Sutherlands 5374
Sutherlands Creek 3331
Sutton 2620
Sutton Forest 2577
Sutton Grange 3448
Svensson Heights 4670
Swan Bay (Coraki) 2471
Swan Bay (Portland) 2324
Swan Hill 3585
Swan Marsh 3249
Swan Reach (SA) 5354
Swan Reach (VIC) 3903
Swan Vale 2370
Swan View 6056
Swanbourne 6010
Swanpool 3673
Swansea (TAS) 7190
Swansea (NSW) 2281
Sweetmans Creek 2325
Swifts Creek 3896
Sydenham (NSW) 2044
Sydenham (VIC) 3038
Sydenham Inlet 3889
SYDNEY CITY 2000
Sydney Airport 2020
Sydney City Street Addresses 2000
Sydney GPO Private Boxes 2001
Sydney University 2006
Sylvania 2224
Symonston 2609
Syndal Via Glen Waverley 3150
Syndal Via Mount Waverley 3149

T

Tabberabbera 3875
Tabbita 2652
Tabilk 3607
Table Cape 7325
Table Top 2640
Tabourie Lake 2539
Tabulam 2470
Tacoma 2259
Taggerty 3714
Tahara 3301
Tahara West 3310
Tahmoor 2573
Taigum 4034
Tailem Bend 5260
Tailem Bend Private Bags 5259
Takone 7325
Talbingo 2720
Talbot 3371
Talbot Brook 6302
Taldra 5311
Taleeban 2669
Talgarno 3691
Tallai 4213
Tallandoon 3700
Tallangatta 3700
Tallarook 3659
Tallebudgera 4228
Tallimba 2669
Tallong 2579
Tallwood 2798
Tally Ho Via Glen Waverley 3150
Tally Ho Via Mount Waverley 3149
Tallygaroopna 3634
Talmalmo 2640
Talwood 4496
Tamarama 2026
Tambar Springs 2381
Tambellup 6320
Tambo 4478
Tambo Crossing 3893
Tambo Upper 3885
Tamborine 4270
Tamleugh 3669
Tamleugh West 3613
Tammin 6409
Tamworth 2340
Tanah Merah 4128
Tandara 3571
Tangalooma 4025
Tangambalanga 3691
Tanilba Bay 2301
Tanja 2550
Tanjil Bren 3833
Tanjil South 3825
Tankerton 3921
Tannum Sands 4680
Tannymorel 4372
Tansey 4601
Tantanoola 5280
Tantaraboo 3764
Tanunda 5352
Tanybryn 3249
Taperoo (SA) 5017
Taplan 5333
Tara 4421
Taradale (NSW) 2653
Taradale (VIC) 3447
Tarago (NSW) 2580
Tarago (VIC) 3818
Tarago River 3831
Taralga 2580
Tarana (NSW) 2787

Taranna (TAS) 7180
Tarcoola 5710
Tarcoon 2839
Tarcowie 5431
Tarcutta 2652
Tardun 6628
Taree 2430
Taren Point 2229
Targa 7257
Tarilta 3451
Tarin Rock 6353
Taringa 4068
Tarlee 5411
Tarnagulla 3551
Tarneit 3030
Taronga 7006
Taronga Park 2088
Taroom 4420
Taroona 7006
Tarpeena 5277
Tarragindi 4121
Tarraleah 7140
Tarranyurk 3422
Tarraville 3971
Tarrawanna 2518
Tarrawarra 3775
Tarrington 3301
Tarro 2322
Tarwin 3956
Tarwin East 3871
Tarwonga 6391
Tascott 2250
Tatana 7251
Tatham 2471
Tathra 2550
Tatong 3673
Tatura 3616
Tatyoon 3378
Taverners Hill 2040
Tawonga 3697
Tawonga Roadside 3691
Tawonga South 3698
Tayene 7257
Taylors Arm 2447
Taylors Lakes 3038
Tea Gardens 2324
Tea Tree Gully 5091
Teatree 7017
Tecoma 3160
Teddington 6324
Teesdale 3328
Telangatuk 3401
Telarah 2320
Telegraph Point 2441
Telfer 6762
Telford 3730
Telita 7254
Telopea 2117
Telopea Downs 3419
Tema 7330
Temora 2666
Tempe (NSW) 2044
Templestowe 3106
Templestowe Heights 3107
Templestowe West 3107
Tempy (VIC) 3489
Tenambit 2323
Teneriffe 4005
Tenindewa 6632
Tennant Creek 5760
Tennyson (Gladesville - NSW) 2111
Tennyson (North Richmond) 2754
Tennyson (QLD) 4105
Tennyson (SA) 5022
Tennyson (VIC) 3572
Tenterden (WA) 6322
Tenterfield 2372
Teralba 2284
Terang 3264
Terara 2540
Teringie 5072
Termeil 2539
Terowie 5421
Terranora 2486
Terrey Hills 2084
Terrigal 2260
Terry Hie Hie 2400
Teutonic 6438
Teven 2480
Tewantin 4565
Tewkesbury 7321
Texas 4385
Thagoona 4306
Thalia 3527
Thallon 4497
Thangool 4716
Tharbogang 2680
Thargomindah 4492
Tharwa (ACT) 2620
The Basin (NSW) 2108
The Basin (VIC) 3154
The Brothers 3900
The Causeway (ACT) 2604
The Channon 2480
The Entrance 2261
The Gap (Brisbane - QLD) 4061
The Gardens (NT) 5790
The Gums (QLD) 4406
The Junction 2291
The Lagoon 2795
The Levels 5095
The Monument 4825
The Narrows (NT) 5790
The Oaks 2570
The Patch 3792
The Risk 2474
The Rock 2655
The Rocks (Sydney) 2000
The Sisters 3265
The Spectacles 6167
The Spit 2088
The Summit 4377
Thebarton 5031
Theodore (ACT) 2905
Theodore (QLD) 4719
Thevenard 5690
Thirlmere 2572
Thirlstane 7307
Thirroul 2515
Thomastown 3074
Thoona 3726
Thora 2454
Thornbury 3071
Thorneside 4158
Thorngate 5082
Thornlands 4163
Thornleigh (NSW) 2120
Thornlie (WA) 6108
Thornton (NSW) 2322
Thornton (VIC) 3712
Thorpdale 3835
Thorpdale South 3824
Thougla 3707
Thredbo Village 2627
Three Bridges 3797
Three Hummock Island 7330
Three Springs 6519
Thulimbah 4376
Thumb Creek 2447
Thurgoona 2640
Thursday Island 4875
Ti Tree (NT) 5751
Tiaro 4650
Tiberias 7120
Tibooburra 2880
Tichborne 2870
Tidal River 3960
Tieri 4709
Tighes Hill 2297
Tilba Tilba 2546
Tilpa 2840
Timboon 3268
Timmsvale 2450
Tin Can Bay 4570
Tinamba 3859
Tinana 4650
Tincurrin 6361
Tinderbox 7152
Tingalpa 4173
Tingha 2369
Tingira Heights 2290
Tingledale 6333
Tingoora 4607
Tinonee 2430
Tintaldra 3708
Tintenbar 2480
Tintinara 5266
Tivoli 4305
Tiwi (NT) 5792
Tocumwal 2714
Togari 7330
Toiberry 7301
Tolga 4882
Tolmie 3723
Tom Price 6751
Tomago 2322
Tomahawk 7254
Tomakin 2537
Tomerong 2540
Tomingley 2869
Toms Creek 2446
Tonebridge 6244
Tongala 3621
Tonganah 7254
Tonghi Creek 3889
Tongio 3896
Tongio West 3898
Tonimbuk 3815
Toobeah 4498
Tooborac 3522
Toodyay 6566
Toogong 2864
Toogoolawah 4313
Toolamba 3614
Toolamba East 3616
Toolangi 3777
Toolbrunup 6320
Toolern Vale 3337
Tooleybuc 2739
Toolibin 6312
Toolijooa 2534
Toolleen 3551
Toolondo 3401
Toolong 3285
Tooma 2642
Toombul 4012
Toongabbie (NSW) 2146
Toongabbie (VIC) 3856
Toonumbar Dam 2474
Toora 3962
Tooradin 3980
Tooradin North 3977
Toorak (VIC) 3142
Toorak Gardens (SA) 5065
Tooraweenah 2831
Toorbul 4510
Toorloo Arm 3909
Toormina 2452
Tooronga Via Glen Iris 3146
Tooronga Via Malvern 3144
Toorooka 2440
Tootgarook 3941
Toowong 4066
Toowoomba 4350
Toowoomba Mc Private Boxes 4352
Toowoon Bay 2261
Torbanlea 4662
Torbay 6330
Toronto 2283
Torquay (QLD) 4657
Torquay (VIC) 3228
Torrens (ACT) 2607
Torrens Creek 4816
Torrens Park 5062
Torrensville 5031
Torrington 2371
Torrita 3490
Torrumbarry 3562
Torwood (QLD) 4066
Tostaree 3888
Tottenham (NSW) 2873
Tottenham (VIC) 3012
Tottenham RAAF (VIC) 3012
Toukley 2263
Towamba 2550
Tower Hill (TAS) 7214
Tower Hill (VIC) 3282
Towlers Bay 2105
Townsville 4810
Townsville Mil. P.O. 4813
Townview 4825
Towong 3707
Towradgi 2518
Towrang 2580
Trafalgar 3824
Tragowel 3579
Trangie 2823
Tranmere (SA) 5073
Tranmere (TAS) 7018
Traralgon 3844
Travencore 3032
Trawalla 3373
Trawool 3660
Trayning 6488
Traynors Lagoon 3478
Treesville 6225
Treeton 6284
Tregeagle 2480
Tregear 2770
Tremont 3785
Trenah 7254
Trentham 3458
Tresco 3583
Tresco West 3584
Trevallyn (NSW) 2421
Trevallyn (TAS) 7250
Trewilga 2869
Triabunna 7190
Trida 2878
Trigg 6029
Trinity Beach 4871
Trinity Gardens 5068
Trott Park 5158
Trowutta 7330
Truganina 3030
Trundle 2875
Trungley Hall 2666
Trunkey Creek 2795
Truro 5356
Tuart Hill 6060
Tubbut 3888
Tucabia 2462
Tucklan 2844
Tuckurimba 2480
Tuena 2583
Tuggerah 2259
Tuggerawong 2259
Tugun 4224
Tulendeena 7254
Tullah 7321
Tullamarine 3043
Tullamore 2874
Tullibigeal 2669
Tullich 3311
Tullochgoram 7214
Tully 4854
Tullymorgan 2463
Tumbarumba 2653
Tumbi Umbi 2261
Tumblong 2729
Tumbulgum 2490
Tumby Bay 5605
Tumoulin 4872
Tumut 2720
Tunbridge 7120
Tuncester 2480
Tuncurry 2428
Tungamah 3728
Tungatinah 7140
Tungkillo 5236
Tunnack 7120
Tunnel 7254
Tunstall 3131
Tunstall Square 3109
Tura Beach 2548
Turill 2850
Turkey Point 6230
Turner (ACT) 2601
Turners Beach 7315
Turners Marsh 7254
Turondale 2795
Tuross Head 2537
Turramurra 2074
Turrawan 2390
Turrella 2205
Turriff 3488
Turtons Creek 3960
Turvey Park 2650
Tusmore 5065
Tutye 3490
Tweed Heads 2485
Tweed Heads South 2486
Twelve Mile 2850
Two Mile Flat 2852
Two Rocks 6037
Two Wells 5501
Tyabb 3913
Tyagarah 2481
Tyalgum 2484
Tyenna 7140
Tyers 3844
Tyers Junction 3825
Tylden 3444
Tyndale Central 2460
Tynong 3813
Tyntynder 3586
Tyrendarra 3285
Tyringham 2453
Tysons Reef 3550

U

Uarbry 2329
Ubobo 4680
Uki 2484
Ulamambri 2357
Ulan 2850
Ulladulla 2539
Ullina 3364
Ulmarra 2462
Ulong 2450
Ultima (VIC) 3544
Ultima East 3586
Ultimo (NSW) 2007
Ulverstone 7315
Umbakumba 5791
Umina 2257
Umina Beach 2257
Unanderra 2526
Undera 3629
Underbool 3509
Undercliffe 2206
Underdale 5032
Underwood (QLD) 4119
Underwood (TAS) 7254
Ungarie 2669
Ungarra 5607
University Of New England (Armidale NSW) 2351

University Of WA
(Crawley) 6009
Unley 5061
Upfield Via Broadmeadows
3047
Upfield Via Campbellfield
3061
Upfield Via Coolaroo 3048
Uplands 3900
Upper Bowman 2422
Upper Esk 7214
Upper Horton 2347
Upper Kalgan 6330
Upper Kedron 4055
Upper Lansdowne 2430
Upper Maffra 3859
Upper Meroo 2850
Upper Morrison 3334
Upper Orara 2450
Upper Plenty 3756
Upper Rouchel 2336
Upper Sturt 5156
Upper Swan 6056
Upper Woodstock 7104
Upper Yarra Dam 3799
Upwey 3158
Uraidla 5142
Uralba 2477
Uralla 2358
Urana 2645
Urangan 4658
Urangeline East 2656
Uranquinty 2652
Urbenville 2475
Uriarra (ACT) 2611
Urisino 2840
Urrbrae 5064
Urunga 2455
Utakarra 6530
Uxbridge 7140

V

Vacy 2421
Vale Park (SA) 5081
Valencia Creek 3860
Valentine 2280
Valley Heights 2777
Valley View (SA) 5093
Varley 6355
Varroville 2565
Vasey (VIC) 3407
Vasse (WA) 6282
Vaucluse 2030
Vaughan 3451
Vectis 3401
Veitch 5312
Venus Bay (SA) 5607
Venus Bay (VIC) 3956
Verdun 5245
Vermont 3133
Verona Sands 7112
Vervale 3814
Victor Harbor 5211
Victoria Estate 4850
Victoria Park (Daylesford)
3460
Victoria Park (VIC) 3067
Victoria Park (WA) 6100
Victoria Park East 6101
Victoria Point 4163
Victoria River Downs 5771
Victoria Valley (TAS) 7140
Victoria Valley (VIC) 3294
View Bank 3084
Villawood 2163
Vincent (QLD) 4814
Vincentia 2540
Vineyard 2765
Vinifera 3591
Violet Town (VIC) 3669
Virginia (QLD) 4014
Virginia (SA) 5120
Vista 5091
Vittoria 2799
Viveash 6056

W

W Tree 3885
Waaia 3637
Waanyarra Rush 3551
Wacol 4076
Waddamana 7030
Wadeye (NT) 5791
Wagaman (NT) 5792
Wagerup 6215
Wagga Wagga (NSW)
2650
Wagga Wagga RAAF 2651
Wagin 6315
Wagoora 4741
Wagstaff Point 2256
Wahgunyah 3687
Wahring 3608
Wahroonga 2076
Waikerie 5330
Waikiki 6169
Wail 3414
Wairewa 3887
Waitara 2077
Waitchie 3544
Wakefield 2301
Wakeley 2176
Wakerley 4154
Wakool 2710
Wal Wal 3381
Walbundrie 2642
Walcha 2354
Walgett 2832
Walgoolan 6422
Walhalla 3825
Walkamin 4872
Walkaway 6528
Walkerston 4751
Walkerville (SA) 5081
Walkerville (VIC) 3959
Walla Walla 2659
Wallabadah 2343
Wallace 3352
Wallacedale 3303
Wallacia 2750
Wallaga Lake 2546
Wallalong 2320
Wallaloo 3381
Wallan Wallan 3756
Wallan Wallan East 3756
Wallangarra (QLD) 4383
Wallangra 2360
Wallarobba 2420
Wallaroo (SA) 5556
Wallaville 4671
Wallendbeen 2588
Wallerawang 2845
Wallgrove 2164
Wallington 3221
Walliston 6076
Walloon 4306
Wallsend 2287
Wallumbilla 4428
Wallup 3401
Walmer (NSW) 2820
Walpa 3866
Walpeup 3507
Walpole 6398
Walwa 3709
Walwa East 3708
Wamberal 2260
Wamboin 2620
Wambool 2795
Wamenusking 6383
Wamoon 2705
Wamuran 4512
Wanaaring 2840
Wanalta 3612
Wanbi 5310
Wandal 4700
Wandana Heights 3216
Wandandian 2540
Wandering 6308
Wandi 6167
Wandiligong 3744
Wandin 3139
Wando Vale 3312
Wandoan 4419
Wandong 3758
Wandsworth 2365
Wang Wauk 2423
Wangan 4871
Wanganella 2710
Wangara 6065
Wangaratta 3677
Wangaratta North 3678
Wangaratta South 3678
Wangary 5607
Wangi Wangi 2267
Wangoom 3279
Wangrabelle 3889
Wanguri (NT) 5792
Wanilla 5607
Wannamal 6505
Wanneroo 6065
Wanniassa (ACT) 2903
Wannon 3301
Wantirna 3152
Wapengo 2550
Waramanga (ACT) 2611
Warana 4575
Waratah (NSW) 2298
Waratah (TAS) 7321
Waratah Bay 3959
Warburton 3799
Warburton Range 6431
Warburton West 3139
Wardell 2477
Wards River 2422
Wareek 3465
Wareemba 2046
Warialda 2402
Warilla 2528
Warkton 2357
Warkworth 2330
Warnbro 6169
Warncoort 3243
Warneet 3980
Warner 4500
Warner Glen 6288
Warners Bay 2282
Warnervale 2259
Warooka 5577
Waroona 6215
Warra 4411
Warrabri 5751
Warrachie 5620
Warracknabeal 3393
Warradale 5046
Warragamba (NSW) 2752
Warragul 3820
Warrah Creek 2339
Warrak 3377
Warramboo 5650
Warrandyte 3113
Warrandyte South 3134
Warrane 7018
Warranwood 3134
Warrawee 2074
Warrawong 2502
Warrego 5760
Warrell Creek 2447
Warren (NSW) 2824
Warrenbayne 3670
Warrenheip 3352
Warrentinna 7254
Warriewood 2102
Warrimoo (Blaxland) 2774
Warringa 7315
Warringah Mall 2100
Warrion 3249
Warriwillah 2429
Warrnambool 3280
Warrow 5607
Warrumbungle 2828
Warwick (QLD) 4370
Warwick (WA) 6024
Warwick Farm (NSW)
2170
Warwick Forward 4371
Wasleys 5400
Watalgan 4670
Watchem 3482
Watchupga 3485
Waterfall 2233
Waterfall Gully 5066
Waterford (QLD) 4206
Waterford (WA) 6152
Waterhouse 7254
Waterloo (NSW) 2017
Waterloo (SA) 5413
Waterloo (TAS) 7116
Waterloo (WA) 6228
Waterloo Corner 5110
Waterloo Plains 3478
Waterman 6020
Watervale 5452
Watheroo 6513
Watson (ACT) 2602
Watsonia 3087
Watsonia Mil Camp 3085
Watsons Bay 2030
Watsons Creek (NSW)
2352
Wattamolla 2535
Wattamondara 2794
Wattle Flat (NSW) 2795
Wattle Glen 3096
Wattle Grove (TAS) 7112
Wattle Grove (WA) 6107
Wattle Hill (TAS) 7172
Wattle Park (SA) 5066
Wattle Park Via Box Hill
(VIC) 3128
Wattle Park Via Surrey Hills
(VIC) 3127
Wattle Vale 3608
Wattleup 6166
Waubra 3352
Wauchope 2446
Waurn Ponds 3221
Wavell Heights 4012
Waverley (NSW) 2024
Waverley (TAS) 7250
Waverton 2060
Wayatinah 7140
Waygara 3888
Wayville 5034
Weatherboard 3352
Webberton 6530
Wedderburn (NSW) 2560
Wedderburn (VIC) 3518
Wee Jasper 2582
Wee Waa 2388
Weeaproinah 3237
Weegena 7304
Weemelah 2407
Weeragua 3889
Weerangourt 3286
Weering 3251
Weerite 3260
Weetah 7304
Weetaliba 2395
Weetangera (ACT) 2614
Weethalle 2669
Weetulta 5573
Weilmoringle 2839
Weipa 4874
Welborough 7254
Welby 2575
Welland 5007
Wellard 6170
Wellcamp 4350
Wellers Hill 4121
Wellingrove 2370
Wellington (NSW) 2820
Wellington Mills 6236
Wellington Point 4160
Wellstead 6328
Welshmans Reef 3462
Welshpool (VIC) 3966
Welshpool (WA) 6106
Wembley 6014
Wembley Downs 6019
Wemen 3549
Wendouree 3355
Wentworth 2648
Wentworth Falls 2782
Wentworthville 2145
Werneth 3352
Werombi 2570
Werona 3364
Werri Beach 2534
Werribee (VIC) 3030
Werrimull 3496
Werrington 2760
Werris Creek 2341
Wesburn 3799
Wesley Vale 7307
West Beach (SA) 5024
West Burleigh 4219
West End (QLD) 4101
West End (WA) 6530
West Fawkner 3046
West Footscray 3012
West Haven 2443
West Heidelberg 3081
West Hoxton 2171
West Lakes 5021
West Lakes Shore 5020
West Lynne 2627
West Melbourne 3003
West Perth 6005
West Pine 7316
West Ryde 2114
West Swan 6055
West Wallsend 2286
West Wyalong 2671
Westall 3169
Westbourne Park 5041
Westbreen 3044
Westbrook (QLD) 4350
Westbury (TAS) 7303
Westdale 2340
Western Camp 3838
Western Creek 7304
Western Junction 7212
Westerway 7140
Westfield 6112
Westgarth 3070
Westgate 2048
Westlake 4074
Westleigh 2120
Westmead 2145
Westmeadows 3049
Westmere 3351
Weston (ACT) 2611
Weston (NSW) 2326
Westonia 6423
Westpoint 2148
Westville 2794
Westwood (QLD) 4702
Westwood (TAS) 7257
Wetherill Park 2164
Wexcombe 6056
Weymouth 7252
Whalan 2770
Whale Beach 2107
Wharminda 5603
Whatley 6053
Wheeler Heights 2098
Wheelers Hill 3150
Wherrol Flat 2429
Whian Whian 2480
Whinstanes 4007
Whiporie 2470
Whitburn 3168
White Cliffs 2836
White Gum Valley 6162
White Hills (TAS) 7250
White Hills (VIC) 3550
White Rock (QLD) 4871
Whitebridge 2290
Whitefoord 7120
Whiteman 6068
Whitemark 7255
Whitemore 7303
Whiteside 4503
Whitfield 3733
Whitfords 6025
Whitlands 3733
Whitsunday 4802
Whittington 3219
Whittlesea 3757
Whitton 2705
Whoorel 3243
Whorouly 3735
Whyalla 5600
Whyalla Jenkins 5609
Whyalla Norrie 5608
Whyalla Playford 5600
Whyalla Stuart 5608
Whyte Yarcowie 5420
Wialki 6473
Wiangaree 2474
Wickepin 6370
Wickham (NSW) 2293
Wickham (WA) 6720
Wickliffe 3291
Widgelli 2680
Wights Mountain 4520
Wihareja 7030
Wilberforce 2756
Wilbinga 6038
Wilby 3728
Wilcannia 2836
Wildes Meadow 2577
Wiley Park 2195
Wilga 6243
Willagee 6156
Willaston 5118
Willatook 3282
Willaura 3291
Willawarrin 2440
Willawong 4110
Willbriggie 2680
Willetton 6155
Williams 6391
Williamsdale 2620
Williamsford 7470
Williamstown (SA) 5351
Williamstown (VIC) 3016
Williamtown (NSW) 2301
Williamtown RAAF (NSW)
2314
Willina 2423
Willmot 2770
Willoughby 2068
Willow Tree 2339
Willowbank 4306
Willowgrove 3825
Willows 4702
Willowvale 4209
Willung 3847
Willung South 3844
Willunga 5172
Wilmington 5485
Wilmot 7310
Wilson (WA) 6107
Wilson (QLD) 4800
Wilson Park 6225

Wilsonton 4350
Wilston 4051
Wilton 2571
Wiltshire 7321
Wiluna 6646
Wimba 3249
Wimbledon 2795
Winchelsea 3241
Windale 2306
Windang 2503
Windaroo 4207
Windermere 7252
Windermere (Claremont TAS) 7011
Windermere (VIC) 3352
Windeyer 2850
Windmill Hill 7250
Windorah 4481
Windsor (NSW) 2756
Windsor (QLD) 4030
Windsor (SA) 5501
Windsor (VIC) 3181
Windsor Gardens 5087
Winegrove 2460
Wingala 2099
Wingan River 3889
Wingello 2579
Wingen 2337
Wingfield 5013
Wingham 2429
Winiam 3418
Winkie 5343
Winkleigh 7251
Winmalee (NSW) 2777
Winnaleah (TAS) 7254
Winnap 3304
Winnellie 5789
Winnindoo 3858
Winslow 3279
Winston Hills 2153
Winthrop 6150
Winton (VIC) 3673
Winton (QLD) 4735
Wirlinga 2640
Wirrabara 5481
Wirrimah 2803
Wirrinya 2871
Wirrulla 5661
Wiseleigh 3885
Wisemans Creek 2795
Wisemans Ferry 2255
Wishart (QLD) 4122
Wishart (VIC) 3189
Wistow 5251
Witchcliffe 6286
Withcott 4352
Withersfield 4702
Wittenoom 6752
Wivenhoe 7320
Woden (ACT) 2606
Wodonga 3690
Wokalup 6221
Wolffdene 4207
Wollar 2850
Wollert 3750
Wollombi 2325
Wollomombi 2350
Wollongbar 2480
Wollongong 2500
Wollongong East (NSW) (Private Boxes Only) 2520
Wollstonecraft 2065
Wollun 2354
Wolseley 5269
Wolumla 2550
Wombarra 2515
Wombat (NSW) 2587
Wombelano 3401
Wombeyan Caves 2580
Womboota 2739
Womerah 3971
Won Wron 3971
Wonboyn Lake 2551
Wondai 4606
Wondalga 2729
Wonga Park 3115
Wongan Hills 6603
Wongarbon 2831
Wongarra 3221
Wongawallen 4210
Wongawilli 2530
Wonthaggi 3995
Wonthella 6530
Wonyip 3962
Wood Wood 3596
Woodanilling 6316
Woodberry 2322
Woodbine 2560
Woodbridge 7162
Woodburn 2472
Woodbury 7120
Woodcroft (SA) 5162
Woodenbong 2476
Woodend 3442
Woodend 4305
Woodfield 3715
Woodford (NSW) 2778
Woodford (QLD) 4514
Woodford (VIC) 3282
Woodford Dale 2463
Woodford Leigh 2463
Woodforde 5072
Woodgate 4660
Woodhill 2535
Woodhouselee 2580
Woodlands 6018
Woodleigh Vale 3989
Woodridge 4114
Woodroofe (NT) 5787
Woods Point 3723
Woodsdale 7120
Woodside (SA) 5244
Woodside (VIC) 3874
Woodstock (NSW) 2793
Woodstock (QLD) 4816
Woodstock (TAS) 7109
Woodstock (VIC) 3751
Woodstock West 3463
Woodstock-On-Loddon 3551
Woodvale (WA) 6026
Woodview 2470
Woodville (NSW) 2321
Woodville (SA) 5011
Woodville Gardens 5012
Woodville North 5012
Woody Point 4019
Woogenilup 6324
Woohlpooer 3408
Wool Bay 5582
Wool Wool 3249
Woolamai 3995
Woolbrook 2354
Woolgoolga 2456
Wooli 2462
Woollahra 2025
Woollahra Park 2029
Woolloomooloo 2011
Woolloongabba 4102
Woolnorth 7330
Woolomin 2340
Woolooga 4570
Woolooma 2337
Woolooware 2230
Wooloowin 4030
Woolsthorpe 3279
Woolwich 2110
Woomargama 2644
Woombye 4559
Woomelang 3485
Woomera 5720
Woongoolba 4207
Woonona 2517
Woorabinda 4702
Wooragee 3747
Wooragee North 3688
Woorak 3418
Woorarra 3962
Woorarra West 3960
Woori Yallock 3139
Woorim 4507
Woorinen 3589
Woorinen South 3588
Woorndoo 3272
Wooroloo 6558
Wooroolin 4608
Woorree 6530
Wootton 2423
World Trade Centre (Melbourne) 3005
Worongary 4213
Woronora 2232
Woronora Dam 2233
Woronora Heights (NSW) 2233
Worsley 6225
Wowan 4702
Woy Woy 2256
Wreck Bay 2540
Wroxham 3889
Wubin 6612
Wudinna 5652
Wulagi (NT) 5793
Wulgulmerang 3885
Wulguru 4811
Wulkuraka 4305
Wundowie 6560
Wunghnu 3635
Wungong 6112
Wurdiboluc 3241
Wurruk 3850
Wurtulla 4575
Wy Yung 3875
Wyadup 6282
Wyalkatchem 6485
Wyalong 2671
Wyandra 4489
Wyanga 2821
Wyangala Dam 2808
Wybong 2333
Wycarbah 4702
Wychbury 2046
Wycheproof 3527
Wychitella 3525
Wye River 3221
Wyee 2259
Wyelangta 3237
Wyena 7254
Wylie Creek 2372
Wyllie 4500
Wynarka 5306
Wyndham (NSW) 2550
Wyndham (WA) 6740
Wyndham Port 6741
Wynn Vale 5127
Wynnum 4178
Wynyard 7325
Wyoming 2250
Wyong 2259
Wyongah 2259
Wyrallah 2480
Wyreema 4352
Wyuna 3620

Y

Yaamba 4704
Yaapeet 3424
Yabba North 3646
Yabula 4816
Yacka 5470
Yackandandah 3749
Yagoona 2199
Yahl 5291
Yalbraith 2580
Yalgogrin North 2669
Yalgoo 6635
Yallah 2530
Yallambie (VIC) 3085
Yalleroi 4702
Yallingup 6282
Yallourn North 3838
Yamanto 4305
Yamba 2464
Yambuk 3285
Yambuna 3621
Yampi Sound 6731
Yan Yean 3755
Yan Yean South 3754
Yanac 3418
Yanakie 3960
Yanchep 6035
Yanco 2703
Yandanooka 6522
Yandaran 4673
Yanderra 2574
Yandilla 4352
Yandina 4561
Yandoit 3461
Yangan 4371
Yangebup 6164
Yaninee 5653
Yankalilla 5203
Yannathan 3981
Yantabulla 2840
Yaouk 2630
Yapeen 3451
Yaraka 4702
Yarck 3719
Yarding 6418
Yarloop 6218
Yarra 2580
Yarra Bay 2036
Yarra Creek 7256
Yarra Glen 3775
Yarra Junction (VIC) 3797
Yarrabah 4871
Yarrabandai 2797
Yarragon 3823
Yarralumla (ACT) 2600
Yarram 3971
Yarram Park 3291
Yarramalong 2259
Yarraman (QLD) 4314
Yarrambat 3091
Yarramundi 2753
Yarrara 3496
Yarraville 3013
Yarrawalla 3575
Yarrawarra (NSW) 2233
Yarrawonga 3730
Yarroweyah 3644
Yarrowitch 2354
Yarrunga (Wangaratta) 3677
Yarwun 4694
Yass 2582
Yatala 4207
Yatala Vale 5126
Yatteyatah 2539
Yea 3717
Yealering 6372
Yearinga 3419
Yeelanna 5632
Yeelirrie 6439
Yeerongpilly 4105
Yelarbon 4388
Yelbeni 6487
Yelgun 2483
Yellingbo 3139
Yenda 2681
Yendon 3352
Yennora 2161
Yeodene 3249
Yeoval 2868
Yeppoon 4703
Yerecoin 6571
Yering 3770
Yerong Creek 2642
Yeronga 4104
Yerrinbool 2575
Yetholme 2795
Yetman 2410
Yilliminning 6312
Yinnar 3869
Yirrigan 6061
Yirrkala 5797
Yokine 6060
Yolla 7325
Yongala 5493
Yoogali 2680
Yooralla Via Balwyn 3103
Yooralla Via Balwyn Nth 3104
York 6302
York Plains 7120
York Town (TAS) 7251
Yorketown (SA) 5576
Yorkeys Knob 4871
Yorkrakine 6409
Yornaning 6311
Yornup 6256
Yoting 6383
Youanmite 3646
Young 2594
Young's Siding 6330
Youngtown 7250
Yowie Bay 2228
Yowrie 2547
Yuendumu 5751
Yulara (NT) 5751
Yuleba 4427
Yulungah 3824
Yumali 5261
Yuna 6532
Yunderup 6208
Yundool 3727
Yungaburra 4872
Yunta 5440
Yuroke 3047
Yuulong 3237

Z

Zamia 6073
Zanthus 6434
Zeehan 7469
Zetland 2017
Zillmere 4034

ANGUS & ROBERTSON PUBLISHERS

Unit 4, Eden Park, 31 Waterloo Road
North Ryde, NSW, Australia 2113, and
16 Golden Square, London W1R 4BN,
United Kingdom

First published in Australia
by Angus & Roberston Publishers in 1987

ISBN 0 207 15617 4

Typeset in 9pt Baskerville by Midland Typesetters
Printed in Australia

ACKNOWLEDGEMENTS

Angus & Robertson Publishers acknowledge the kind assistance given in the assembling of this Companion. Our sincere thanks are extended in particular to Jo Monie of the Stamps and Philatelic Branch of Australia Post, to Don Darbyshire and Vann Cremer of Australia Post whose private postcard collections were put at our disposal and to Barry Watts for compiling the text.

The illustrations used on page 10 *Stage Coach, Royal Mail* by Arthur Esam, page 19 *Attacking the Mail* by S. T. Gill, page 27 *Lighthouse, Port Jackson* by S. T. Gill, and page 57 *Native Wildflowers* by Louisa Ann Meredith are used with permission of the National Library of Australia.

The illustration on page 15 *Gold Diggers Receiving a Letter from Home* by William Strutt is used with the permission of the Art Gallery of New South Wales.

The illustration on page 41 *The Arrival of the Post* by B. Warwick is used with the permission of the Mitchell Library, Sydney, and that used on page 25 is from the Emma Minnie Boyd Sketchbook published by the National Gallery, Canberra.

The publishers would like to thank Heinemann Publishers Australia Pty Ltd for permission to use an extract from *The Fortunes of Richard Mahony* by Henry Handel Richardson. "Air Mail—Palestine" by David McNicoll is reproduced with the permission of the author.

"Come-By-Chance" by A. B. Paterson, "The Mails" by Will Lawson, "The Postman" by C. J. Dennis, "The Travelling Post Office" by A. B. Paterson and extracts from *The Letters of Rachel Henning* by Rachel Henning, *The Letters of Norman Lindsay* by Norman Lindsay and *We of the Never-Never* by Mrs Aeneas Gunn are used with the permission of Angus & Robertson Publishers.